Worried All the Time

Overparenting in an Age of Anxiety and How to Stop It

DAVID ANDEREGG, Ph.D.

Free Press

NEW YORK   LONDON   TORONTO
SYDNEY   SINGAPORE

*f*P
FREE PRESS
A Division of Simon & Schuster, Inc.
1230 Avenue of the Americas
New York, NY 10020

FREE PRESS and colophon are trademarks
of Simon & Schuster Inc.

For information regarding special discounts for bulk purchases,
please contact Simon & Schuster Special Sales
at 1-800-456-6798 or business@simonandschuster.com

Manufactured in the United States of America

1   3   5   7   9   10   8   6   4   2

LIBRARY OF CONGRESS CATALOGING-IN-PUBLICATION DATA
Anderegg, David.
Worried all the time : overparenting in an age of anxiety
and how to stop it / David Anderegg.
p.   cm.
Includes bibliographical references and index.
1. Parenting—Psychological aspects.   2. Anxiety.
3. Anxiety in children.   I. Title.
HQ755.8.A53   2003
649'.1—dc21   2003040867

ISBN 0-7432-2568-6

ACKNOWLEDGMENTS

Many people helped this book find its way into the world. Among the most helpful early on was Henry Meininger, my editor and friend, who first gave me an opportunity to write about children for an audience outside my immediate professional family. Gareth Esersky has also been a sensitive and judicious guide who has helped me find a place from which to speak.

Rachel Klayman and Elizabeth Stein, my editors at Free Press, have been unwavering in their attempts to rescue me from my own excesses of word and argument.

Rob Peterson, the Head of Berkshire Country Day School, and his extraordinary teaching staff have welcomed me into a community dedicated to the task of thinking clearly about children and what they need, and I am grateful for their embrace. I am also deeply grateful to the "hearts" of BCD, Gwen Connolly, Sandie Taylor, and Jennifer Drees.

I am indebted to my encouragers at Bennington College, including Steven Bach, David Rees, and especially April Bernard, an unswerving literary conscience and an extraordinary teacher and friend.

My thinking about children and families has been influenced by many colleagues, especially my friend Jane Sobel, whose wise counsel about child therapy has been invaluable over many years. Most of all, I wish to thank my wife, Kelley DeLorenzo, who never fails to astonish me with her depth and sophistication in our unending conversations about children.

This book is dedicated with love to
Robert and Anita Anderegg,
my first teachers

CONTENTS

Introduction. Whose Zeitgeist Is It, Anyway?   1

One. Nervous Wrecks:
Scenes from the Front Lines   17

Two. Dr. Schreber and Mrs. Jellyby:
The Myth of Scientific Parenting   37

Three. The Management of Worrying:
Therapeutic Traditions   63

Four. Oh, Those Nasty Date Books   81

Five. Trouble in Au-Pairadise   103

Six. Do As I Say, Not As I Did   127

Seven. Who's Afraid of the Big Bad Culture?   151

Eight. When Columbine Was Only a Flower   173

Nine. But What About Them?   193

Notes   213
Index   222

CONTENTS

Introduction

WHOSE ZEITGEIST
IS IT, ANYWAY?

As a therapist, my job is to ask questions. It is what I do all day long. My patients, both children and adults, sometimes have surprising answers for my questions, but there is one that no one has been able to answer to my satisfaction. The question is: why are contemporary American parents so worried about their children?

The way I ask this question usually goes something like this: "Your children are smart, healthy, and cute; your family is fairly well-off; there are no huge storm clouds on this horizon . . . so, what are you so worried about?" The more general form of the question, however, is: why, even in times of relative peace and relative plenty, do American parents worry so much about their kids?

One simple answer to this question is: Parents have always worried about their kids. That's what parents do. It is in the nature of parents of every species to protect and foster their young, and since that's their job, that's the thing they worry about the most. There is a reason why a protective mother used to be called a mother hen: hens do the same thing, protecting and worrying about their chicks.

But hens have a pretty hard life, compared with most of us. Keeping their chicks fed and protected requires, of hens, enormous amounts of energy. My question is why, since keeping children alive, fed, and protected from danger seems to be a lot easier for us than for most other animals and certainly a lot easier for us than for most parents in all of human history, do parents now worry so much? Why does it *feel* so hard?

Here we come to the first big bump in this long and bumpy road: the history question. Is it true that we worry more than others have worried, or that we worry *too much?* The answer to that question depends upon how one reads the zeitgeist. I believe we do worry more than parents used to worry, and we worry more than we need to. Of course, I am a person to whom people bring their worries. If I were a rock star or a field botanist I might not have this point of view, but parents' worries are what I encounter daily, and the experience I bring to this project is twenty years' worth of parents' questions.

One could argue, then, that as a child therapist, my view of the zeitgeist is necessarily skewed. Since I consult all day long with people who are by definition *patients,* my view of normal family life must be distorted. However, as a psychologist who consults to an elementary school and a psychologist who regularly lectures about normal development to groups of parents of supposedly normal kids, I also come into contact with large numbers of parents whose children are not in treatment and do not need to be in treatment. And these parents are just as worried as the parents of my child patients.

Where else do I get my data about the zeitgeist? I belong to the great American club of parent commiserators. As a father of two children who are now young adults, I have spent years with my siblings and friends sitting around the dinner table or the supermarket aisle talking about topic A: our worries about our own children. My siblings and friends know I am a child therapist, so here, too, I probably get more than my share of uncensored worries, and more than my share of appeals for free advice. But my reading of my peers is that we're a pretty worried group. From my days as a parent in a parent-cooperative day care center (when the worries were about vaccinations and ear infections and, most of all, toilet training) to my days sitting in the applying-to-college meetings at my children's high school (when the worries were about aiming too high or landing too low), I have seen a lot of people obsessing about precisely how to do the best for their children.

A simple example: I am frequently asked if I believe that it is good parenting to allow children to play with toy guns. As a consultant to schools, I am exposed to many environments where toy guns are not allowed. I have met many families, in clinical settings and in casual contexts, who do not allow children to play with toy guns. I am well aware of the arguments on both sides: I do not believe that there is anything wrong with fantasy aggression, but I am certainly aware that a realistic-looking toy gun in the wrong setting can get a person killed by someone who feels threatened by what is thought to be a real gun. The banning, or not, of toy guns raises the following questions, all of which I have been asked to consider in the last two decades:

Are toy guns ever okay? Are nonrealistic guns, like ray guns, better than toy guns that look like real guns? What about squirt guns? If toy guns are not okay, what should I do when my child holds up his thumb and index finger and says, "Bang-bang"? Where did he get that idea, anyway? What about bows and arrows? Are they okay? My son's friend has a BB gun—should I allow him to go over there? Is target shooting okay? What about paintball—is paintball okay? My son was raised to believe that guns are not okay. He was asked to go to a party where people will be playing paintball. What should I do? My son wants to be a cowboy on Halloween, and he says cowboys carry pistols. Now what? He went to a six-year-old's birthday party, and they watched a violent movie. Should I allow him to go back there?

Can I ask his best friend's parents to put away the toy guns when my son is coming over? Will they think he is an oddball and ostracize him? Or should I just keep him home?

This is the phenomenon I call overparenting. These decisions all seem critical, but there are so many of them to make that it is easy for parents to feel overwhelmed. The choices have a tendency to multiply into an infinitude of decisions that seem like they might determine the course of our children's lives. The "over" part of overparenting is just this: overthinking, overworrying, and eventually, overacting on the decisions arrived at in a worried state. Overparenting is trying to make perfect decisions every single time, in a world that is much more indeterminate and forgiving than most parents believe.

The people who have asked me these questions about toy guns are all trying to be the best parents they can be. But I also know that this level of complex worrying was simply not present when I was a kid. No child I grew up with had to deal with these issues, and no parent I knew then ever bothered with these questions. Whether this means they didn't worry enough or that we worry too much is an open question, but the direction seems clear: contemporary parents worry a lot more than parents in the relatively recent past.

❈   ❈   ❈

My other major source of data about the temper of the times is my consumption of a large quantity of the stuff dished up by the contemporary media culture. It is clear that many parents, certainly the ones I know, are voracious media consumers, and for one simple reason: they are always trying to figure out what problems everyone else is having, and what to do about them. The insularity of the nuclear family—the fact that we no longer live in extended communities where everyone knows firsthand what is going on in everyone else's family—makes parents desperate to find out the answers to their own urgent question: is my child *normal?* Since we do not live in longhouses, and therefore have no direct experience of other people's families, we need to read magazines or newspapers to tell us what other people's children are doing. It is one of the few ways of finding out whether what theirs are doing is as alarming as what our own are doing.

But there is a problem with using the media culture as a source of normative data: it is pretty clear that in a competitive media culture, a certain amount of exaggeration is necessary to get a busy reader's attention. As I sometimes say to parents, I wish I had a dollar for every time I have read, in the last ten years, the words "children" and "crisis" in the same sentence. I'd be set for life. The formula for the typical child-in-crisis article is to collect some scary anecdotes about what some kids are up to, and to overplay the data as if to suggest that this behavior is, somehow, the new norm. A good example is an article with the lurid title "The Sex Lives of Your Children," by Lucinda Franks, which appeared in the February 2000 issue of *Talk* magazine. Although most research data, even the data quoted by Franks herself in the body of her article, controverted her claim that "they're all doing this now," the tone of the article makes the claim that outrageous sexual behavior is now the norm. Or how about the article by Ron Powers featured on the cover of the March 2002 issue of the *Atlantic Monthly,* the one that tells the story of two teenaged murderers in Vermont but that is called "The Apocalypse of Adolescence"? This trend is consistent with the tabloidization of news in general: every petty crime is now a scandal and every thunderstorm a disaster, so it should not be surprising that news about children has gone the same way. Just as research has demonstrated over many years that big consumers of television news are likely to make errors in predicting the likelihood of violence affecting their lives, so we might expect that media consumers fed on a diet of children-in-crisis stories will overestimate the degree of crisis our children are facing; we would certainly expect such people to be more worried about raising their children than their parents were.

I sometimes enrage parents by describing myself as a "crisis agnostic." I do not believe that American children are in crisis, with one important exception: for the 17 percent of American children who live in families with annual incomes below the poverty line, life is a constant crisis.* Malnutrition, lack of access to health care, disorganized or chaotic living arrangements, substandard housing: all these things constitute a genuine crisis for children who live in poverty. If our society wants to do something about that crisis, I'm all for it. But if we use the language of crisis every time we describe *all* children, we debase language and we increase everyone's mistrust of behavioral science by claiming that there is a crisis that does not exist. The issue is the difference between what we *want* for our children and what they *need* . . . and there *is* a difference.

For example, we were recently engaged in a national frenzy about bullying and teasing. *People* magazine trumpeted on its cover a story entitled "Bullies: The Disturbing Epidemic Behind School Violence." Well, if it's an epidemic, we'd better do something about it right away, because it will just . . . spread, as epidemics tend to do. But is bullying a crisis? Is it even a new development? Skeptics—and there are many in this discussion—point out that bullying and teasing are old news: we have always tolerated a certain amount of unfairness, or the strong taking from the weak, among our children. If we now wish to change this, if we now wish to stop tolerating this kind of unfairness, we may choose to do so because our values are changing, and that may be a very good thing. But we do not need to invent a crisis or insist that our policies *must* change because of the latest epidemic. If we wish to change our approach to children, we can do so without manufacturing an emergency. But the headline SOME NOW WISH TO STOP PHYSICAL INTIMIDATION, A CENTURIES-OLD PRACTICE AMONG CHILDREN makes for far less dramatic reading.

* The U.S. government placed this figure at $13,290 for a family of three in 1999.

My goal is to accomplish a reasonable level of concern without adding to the tabloidization of children. So, while I know that parental worrying is widespread, I make no claims that parental worrying is a crisis *for children*. I think our children will survive having a bunch of worrywarts for parents. I do have some intuitions from clinical work about how all this worrying will affect our children, but the effects of parental worrying on our children are far from clear (I return to this topic in Chapter 9). My point is that, if parents are suffering needlessly, this in itself is a problem that we can try to alleviate. If this book helps parents sleep better at night, I will have achieved my goal; and if our children thrive as a result of their parents' getting a good night's sleep, so much the better.

THE WORRIED PARENT: WHAT ARE THE FACTS?

Are parents more worried today than they used to be? The nonprofit public information organization Public Agenda conducted a national telephone poll in December 1998 that asked the following question: "Do you think it's much harder or much easier for parents to do their jobs these days, or do you think that it's about the same?" Of the randomly selected respondents, 78 percent said that it is much harder for parents to do their jobs, compared with 4 percent who said it is much easier. This feeling rings true with reports I hear from parents I meet every day, but we don't really know for sure: it might be the case that parents have always felt that raising kids at *this* time is harder than it used to be. Public Agenda has noted that data demonstrating historical trends is almost impossible to find, because no one seems to have been gathering data on this question until the last few years. There has not been a sense, until recently, that parental worrying is outside the range of normal; while there have always been individuals who have been worriers, described in the old days as overprotective mothers, the sense that the norms have changed is very recent. In my clinical work, I know the norms have changed: questions from parents that used to be unusual are now routine.

Social policies designed to protect children seem to have had no effect on helping parents feel less worried. Children are now affected by volumes of safety regulations that were absent even in very recent years. I am old enough to remember when cars did not have seat belts, and even when they were present, their use was not required when many of us were children. Bicycle helmets are now becoming standard, as well as helmets when kids are skiing. Childproof medicine bottles are not all that old, historically; flameproof pajamas and safety labels on toys also are now taken for granted, but are relatively recent. While these safety practices really do save lives, they don't put us at ease; in fact, they may have the opposite effect. One might argue that the invention of childproof medicine bottles and kid-size bicycle helmets should *decrease* parental worrying and make contemporary parents feel calmer than parents in previous generations, but this does not appear to be the case.

MAKING WORRYING GO AWAY

The treatment of worrying* is relatively complicated, but there is one point upon which most reasonable people might agree: it never helps a worrier to tell them, "Stop worrying!" or, "What're you getting so worked up for?" or, "Lighten up!" Saying things like this might make the speaker feel better, but

---

* Throughout this book, I will use the commonsense term "worrying" to denote the more widespread form of this activity, and the more clinical term "anxiety" to denote the more pathological form of this activity. One needs to bear in mind that the border between these two conditions may be in the eye of the beholder: just as one person's passionate interest may be, to a family member, psychotic monomania, so one person's normal worrying may be, to that person's spouse or child, intractable mental illness.

the admonition itself has absolutely no effect. If the worrier could stop that easily, he or she would have stopped long ago; most worriers say to themselves, several thousand times per day, *Stop worrying so much!* Chastising worriers as a form of treatment is not really treatment at all. It is just thinly disguised aggression. What this admonition does is shame the sufferer into silence. Today's worried parent has received this kind of response from the culture at large: parents who are worried, and therefore "overinvolved" with their children, are ridiculed, which does not help them feel less worried or overprotective, but may make them shut up.

The lighter side of this form of shaming is contemporary humor, and humor about worried parents can be funny, especially if you're not a parent. Jon Katz, in his Suburban Detective novels, offers up this type of social commentary in his invented New Jersey suburb of Rochambeau, a world where children get nicknames (behind their backs) like Rachel Isn't Ready, as in "Rachel isn't ready for overnights/PG-13 movies/cable/9 P.M. bedtimes/books that aren't about cats or Native American myths." Here's Katz on the subject of Camp Night at the local elementary school:

> Around me, the questions swirled: "Are the boys allowed in the girls' camp? In the cabins? Is the exercise too strenuous? Are bedtimes enforced? Are kids allowed to bring pets/candy/Gameboys/Walkmen? How many visiting days? Are there any wild animals? Have there ever been any wild animals? Have wild animals ever bitten any of the campers?"

At the darker end of the spectrum are the vitriolic attacks upon contemporary parents that appear regularly in print media. Consider, for example, a review of new parenting magazines written by David Kamp in the June 2000 issue of *GQ* magazine. In a three-page outpouring of spleen, Kamp attacks contemporary parents for being concerned about parenting.

This "Oh, my God, we're parents!" self-consciousness seems to be the way of the parenting world today, trickling down into the attitudes of post-boomer moms and dads. In his keynote address in the premiere issue of *Offspring*, Steven Swartz . . . argues that being a parent is harder now than it used to be. By the time his toddler son is 4 or 5, Swartz argues, "my wife and I will need to be experts on the new school choices—charter, magnet, at-home . . . And, like many parents, we do have a computer in the home, but we're not exactly sure what we or James should be doing with it." Well, boo-f*cking-hoo! Sure, the social context is different and the new technology has scary implications, but can it really be harder for parents now than it was when the nation wasn't so amazingly prosperous, when there were both hot and cold wars on, when diapers weren't disposable, when there wasn't *Sesame Street* and *The Lion King* and Nickelodeon to turn to whenever respite was needed?

If the purpose of this article was to help parents be less anxious, my guess is it failed. People who are anxious are never helped by being ridiculed. If the purpose of this article is *not* to help people change their behavior, I suppose it is meant to entertain in the way that Mencken used to entertain: by inviting the reader to join the writer in feeling superior to the fool who was the butt of the joke. As a big fan of Mencken, I can get with this program, but it is not to be mistaken for a worry remedy: ridicule does nothing for the worried parent except make him or her feel angry . . . and more isolated.

It needs to be said at the outset that this is not what this book is about. Making fun of people who worry too much yields little in terms of understanding the worrying, and yields even less as a form of therapy. Understanding excessive worrying requires that we set aside the moralistic tone usually reserved for such discussions; it doesn't help a worrier to be reflective when he or she is attacked for being spoiled, foolish, or self-indulgent. And it requires a little bit of effort to keep in mind that excessive worrying is something that causes *suffering* in parents: suffering that is both unnecessary *and also very real.* It may be that thinking about the big picture—the world outside the immediate family—is a necessary moral action *and* an effective treatment for worrying. But the question I want to address is, why is that so hard to do now?

THE WORLD AFTER SEPTEMBER 11

For Americans, the events of September 11, 2001, were a watershed in our history. The tragedies of that day changed the way Americans experienced their own worries, and their worries about their children, at least for a while. In my discussion of the events of September 11, I distinguish between people directly affected by the terrorist attacks, those who lost loved ones (including the children who lost parents), and those who were traumatized by witnessing terrible events. Certainly one could make a case for a massive case of post-traumatic stress disorder, in the sense that many of us watched the events unfolding in real time via national news media. But for those who were present at the scene and witnessed firsthand things that many of us did not, the trauma was, and will always be, of an intensity that the rest of us can experience only in nightmares.

As a child therapist living and working three hours from New York City, I was called on that day and in the days that followed to process, with my patients, those tragic events. Most people I worked with had not lost a loved one or witnessed the calamities directly. For us, at a little remove from the action, the question on everyone's mind was how to explain this to our children. I was asked, like thousands of other child experts, to advise parents on how to speak to their children about the unspeakable, and my advice was much the same as other child experts': let them know adults will do everything they can to protect them, help them feel safe as best you can, and limit ex-

posure to traumatic visual images. As a child expert who partici-
pates in what is sometimes a Tower of Babel of competing or
conflicting advice, I was cheered to see the virtual unanimity
in what we, as a community of child experts, were advising. The
children in my community had their questions answered, and
settled down to some sense of normalcy pretty quickly. The
parents I know were much more worried than usual, but, of
course, worried about different things.

The changes in the atmosphere were profound, but also
transient. And the changes in the atmosphere taught extraordinary things about our lives as parents, especially about our
experience of control. The initial terrorist attacks were, after
all, attacks on adults, and adults and children were momen-
tarily joined in concern about their mutual safety. In my own
practice, children's concerns about parents' safety in the days
following the attacks were at least as common as parents' concerns about children's safety. The usual asymmetry of these
concerns—that is, we, the parents, have all the power and make
all the important decisions, and they, the children, benefit or
suffer from our actions—was temporarily suspended. We were
all, for a time, children: helpless and powerless in the face of
forces way beyond our control or understanding.

I observed, in the parents I know, a curious sense of relief from worry, side by side with the profound worries about
everyone's safety. The life-or-death quality of many issues that
confronted people in those weeks made all the previous worries seem less important, but the lack of personal control over
events also made for a change in the kind of worrying we were
all doing. As we now know, in the weeks immediately after September 11, many adults spent a little more time living in the
present: wine collectors started consuming their wine collec-
tions; people started smoking again; people stopped working
so hard on the future and started spending a little more time
enjoying the present. There was even a baby boomlet nine
months later, although we do not know if that was due to people getting going on their deferred goal of parenting or simply

taking a little extra time to enjoy the present moment. Parents, too, took a little mental vacation: many parents I knew stopped worrying about homework or television, and enjoyed a short respite from limit setting and decision making.

These changes proved to be short-lived. But the changes demonstrated the immense effect that personal control has over our own sense of well-being. When the power and control was largely held by others (in this case, terrorists or the U.S. government), parents I knew were very anxious about their children's safety. But there was a less-advertised shift toward relief from worry: since real survival was at stake for many people, all of a sudden SAT scores and navel rings, and what to do about them, became much less important. And as the sense of threat to personal survival receded, all these parenting decisions, and the worry that accompanies them, came charging back.

OVERVIEW OF THE BOOK

In the chapters that follow, I will be attempting to address the question of parental worrying: Why now, and why so much? And what can we do about it? The earlier part tells some stories of real parents and provides some ideas from social science research about why parents now are more worried than ever before. I also summarize what we already know about parenting, and explain why the engineering solution to parenting (that is, figuring out how to parent by acquiring more scientifically based knowledge) is a fatally flawed approach. This part ends with a look at psychological theories about worrying and the treatment for worrying they suggest. Although these treatments were devised for clinical populations, they can give us plenty of insight into why we worry so much and what to do about it.

In the later part of this book, I take a look at some specific worries that keep parents awake at night. These topics are not comprehensive—there is always more to worry about than can be catalogued. But these topics are common worries that our own parents didn't even think about, things like overscheduling children (Chapter 4), substitute care (Chapter 5), experimentation with drugs and problems with authority (Chapter 6), the effects of exposure to media culture (Chapter 7), and school violence (Chapter 8). Not all of these topics apply to children of every age; while the worries about the effects of media culture span almost the entire range of childhood and adolescence, some of the topics lean toward earlier years (substitute care) and some lean toward the later years (experimentation with drugs). But each topic tells us something about ourselves as parents . . . indeed, most of these worries tell us more about ourselves as parents than about the real lives of our children.

At the end of the later chapters there is a section entitled "Try This at Home." When acting as a therapist, I am reluctant to tell people what to do; asking questions suits my style infinitely better. I am, however, comfortable asking people to consider something—a concept, a feeling, a fact—that may help them decide what to do on their own. This is the pattern I attempt to follow when I suggest, "try this at home." I do not pretend to have all the answers to cure parental worrying—there are no easy answers anyway. Some of the suggestions in "Try This at Home" may appear to be fanciful, but that's what imagination is all about. Imagining things differently is the best cure for worrying—which, after all, is the point of this book in the first place.

In the last chapter I consider the effects of parental worrying on our society, on our children, and on ourselves. This research has not been done, the facts aren't in—we don't really know for sure. So this last chapter is necessarily speculative, based upon my work with families and my own intuition about the children I have known. If the speculation fits your experience, I will consider myself successful in reading your zeitgeist as well as my own. If not, not . . . we must be talking to different people. In that case, I hope the speculations are an entertaining view into a parallel universe of children and families.

Whatever universe we are in, we're still all in this together. Bringing up the next generation is serious business but, I hope to show, not deadly business. There is room for error, room for pigheadedness, room for laughter—much more room than most of us believe. I hope to help parents, and people who know and worry about worried parents, to find some room in these pages to breathe a little more easily.

One

NERVOUS WRECKS: SCENES FROM THE FRONT LINES

Some true stories of worried parents, from my own experience:

A mother of a second-grader asks to meet with the consulting child therapist. She is concerned about whether her daughter is safe at school. When asked to describe the problem, she reports that she is concerned about a little boy in her daughter's class because the boy "looks mean." "What do you mean, he looks mean?" asks the confused therapist. "Well, he looks like he could hurt somebody . . . and he did hit another child in the class last year." "And . . . ?" "And I'm worried that he might become violent. What if he hurt my daughter? Do you think we should be home-schooling her? At least at home, we'll know she's safe."

A father calls an elementary school teacher at home on a school night because he is very concerned about his son's account of his day at school. His son said that he had been practicing a joke to tell his classmates, and when he told the joke, his classmates didn't laugh. The father is concerned; he asks the teacher to explain what's going on in this classroom. The teacher, flummoxed, has little to say. The father wonders why the classroom environment is so unsupportive and why peers feel the need to hurt one another's feelings. He goes on to voice concerns about his son's self-esteem and expresses the wish that if his son is going to all the trouble to practice a joke, the teacher would somehow ensure that the other kids will laugh.

The therapist consults with a father of a first-grader, who is very worried about his son. It seems that a friend at school pulled down his own pants and showed his son his penis. "And . . . ?" asks the confused child therapist. "Well, first off, I want to know if this is sexual abuse. Should I call the Department of Social Services and report that this child is in trouble? I thought it was true that kids who sexually abuse other kids are being abused themselves. If he's being abused, the authorities need to be notified." While the therapist struggles with how to respond to this concern, the father continues: "Of course, the main reason I'm here is to line up therapy for my son. I don't want him to suffer from the effects of this trauma."

❖   ❖   ❖

These stories are all true, and they are typical of the kinds of worries I deal with every day as a child therapist. In each case the story reveals much about the parent and very little about the child. In none of these cases was the child symptomatic, or suffering in any profound way as a result of the injury or problem he or she had sustained. The suffering was all on the part of the parents, who really were suffering, with a great deal of worry about their children's emotional health.

In each of these anecdotes there is a curious mixture of old and new worries, but one can definitely hear contemporary themes in the near background. These parents are all well-educated people who read and think a great deal about their children and what they need, and so they are alert to the apparent dangers inherent in modern life. In the first story, the worried mother is up against competing priorities: she wants to be a good member of a school community, but her child's safety comes first. The real worry here, the bottom line, is "My child will be killed in school." She is not saying this, exactly, but she is saying something like this, or feeling it: great harm might come to her child now, and of course, if the potentially dangerous second-grader is still around in subsequent years, her child could get killed.

No parent wants her child to be injured at school, but this level of worry might be experienced as something slightly over the top. This level of concern, and the seriousness with which it is addressed, is certainly a change from the ethos of schools of my own childhood, when a certain amount of physical aggression was seen as the stuff of life. The unspoken worry, that my child will be killed at school, would, in another era, be seen as pathological separation anxiety: the magical belief that a parent's presence is the only thing that keeps a child alive, and without that physical presence, the child, or the parent, will die. Now this worrying is frequent enough that we have to see it as something else. I see it as post-Columbine worry: the unfounded belief that something I saw on television is, because of its vividness, a very likely threat. The jump from "If it happened there, it could happen here, too," to "It happened there, so it is likely to happen here, too," is made in a fraction of a second.

In the second example, the father's worry is, on the surface, easy to dismiss: if a joke isn't funny, it's not funny, and no amount of intervention on the part of the teacher will change that fact. But the background worry is very real, and very much alive: my child will feel bad about himself because he failed. It is true that the excesses of the self-esteem movement have been addressed in educational circles, and some of the more egregious curricular developments of the self-esteem movement have been toned down; we see less and less of the "It's so wonderful to be me" curriculum that was so popular in the late eighties and early nineties. But the worries about a child's self-esteem are still very present in the national parent community.

It is painful, and always has been, to see one's child fail at anything, even something as simple as telling a funny joke; but it is more critical if the long-term deleterious effects of low self-esteem put the child at risk for school failure, drug abuse, and the like. The worry behind the father's complaint might be expressed as something like this: "If he feels like a failure, he will become a failure." While a conservative parenting adviser might suggest the vital importance of failure (something like "If he feels like a failure, next time he will try harder and learn to be a success"), contemporary parents are not completely in the wrong here. Most parents I encounter are very well schooled in the language, supported by sound scientific research, of the self-fulfilling prophecy, and this research, now two decades old and showing no signs of wear, suggests that feeling like a success is a big part of succeeding. Armed with such knowledge, the father in our second example might feel he has a right to worry when his child fails, and a right to insist that the teacher not allow this to happen. Schools, especially schools for younger children, should be places where children succeed, so they can feel good about themselves and build on their history of success—right?

Our third example requires little in the way of explanation. In previous generations, playing doctor, or mutual sexual exploration, was never welcomed by parents but was expected and tolerated to a certain degree. Freud's explication of the sexual life of children was never completely accepted, but it did much to move children's efforts to satisfy their sexual curiosity out of the realm of moral evil. The decade of the eighties, complete with riveting news reports of sexual abuse at day care centers and lawsuits regarding recovered memories of childhood sexual abuse, gave parents a twenty-year nightmare from which many have yet to wake. The long-term effects of sexual abuse, including lifelong emotional difficulties, are real, and what parent would not want to be vigilant about preventing a lifetime of emotional difficulty? As teachers and professionals, we might be comfortable saying that a child's showing his penis to another child at school is not sexual abuse, but in any domain where the boundaries are murky and the stakes are high, why take a chance?

In each of these examples we can see the faint, or sometimes not so faint, markings of old waves of national anxiety. In most of these cases, the wave of anxiety has come and gone, at least in the realm of official knowledge and recommendation, but the echoes of the wave linger for decades in the area where we are most vulnerable to primitive and irrational thinking: our children. Child experts, of course, are the ones responsible for this ebb and flow of parental worrying, since we were the ones who got everybody all worked up in the first place. But then, when we have figured out how to manage the new scary phenomenon, we tell everybody to calm down. I call this the Emily Litella syndrome, named for the old Gilda Radner character on *Saturday Night Live*. Miss Litella, as you may recall, was a concerned citizen on the "Weekend Update" section of the show who would work herself into a froth of righteous indignation about an imagined social problem; when she was finally corrected, she would say with a smile, "Never mind." Unfortunately, child development experts often act the same way.

Take the example of *bonding*, the wave of national anxiety that predated all our current examples. The national obsession with bonding between a mother and an infant in the moments after birth was begun in an interesting, poorly controlled, and admittedly exploratory piece of research published by pediatricians Marshall Klaus and John Kennell in 1976. The research purported to demonstrate that children who had an opportunity to bond with their mothers in the moments immediately after birth had better developmental outcomes than children who were not able to bond. The widespread anxiety caused by these findings led to considerable soul-searching in the childbirth community, and also had a dramatic effect on medical practice. The fashion of the previous decades, to knock mothers out during the birth process with general anesthesia, was largely abandoned so that mothers could be awake and alert for the moments of bonding that were supposed to be so critically important to the newborn infant.

While these developments were salutary (and I, for one, certainly do not mean to suggest a return to the good old days of anesthetized mothers), the facts of bonding research turned out to be illusory at best. The initial study was a methodological disaster, and it failed to meet even minimal criteria to establish facts in the way scientists understand them. The obsession with mother-infant bonding was more or less officially ended, *in the scientific community,* with the publication of Diane Eyer's 1992 book, *Mother-Infant Bonding,* which completely discredited the Klaus and Kennell research, therefore obviating any recommendations that might have followed from it. Indeed, Eyer demonstrated that the research was so flawed and the recommendations so contaminated by prejudice about the role of women in child rearing that she suggested that the term "bonding" should be completely eliminated from national discourse.

But is the anxiety about bonding gone? Not completely. I still hear occasional worries about bonding with newborns, although sometimes younger parents have been affected by talking with their somewhat older friends who were new parents at the peak of the bonding craze. And Eyer's wishes notwithstanding, the word remains a staple of popular parenting publications. For example, the June/July 2001 issue of *Parenting* magazine announces a story by shouting on its cover: "Bonding with your baby: what every Dad needs to know." Although the focus of the article, and many like it, is now on the importance of the bonding experience for parents, not for children, it still carries the clear message that bonding, as soon as possible after birth, is a critical experience that parents *must* have with their infants. Diane Eyer's work, and the actual disclaimers of the centrality of bonding by Drs. Klaus and Kennell themselves, have done nothing to stop the bonding movement from living its own freewheeling life.

Child development professionals expect parents to be rational when it comes to their children, but we often forget that it is precisely in thinking about their children that people are most likely to be emotional at best and irrational at worst. The many waves of national anxiety that have passed since the bonding wave—including the sexual abuse wave, the self-esteem wave, and the school violence wave—have receded or will recede in the professional community as new evidence comes in that tempers the passions incited by the first findings. Sexual abuse is prevalent, much more prevalent than people thought in the fifties, and this finding appears to be robust. It does not appear that we will discover sexual abuse to be less prevalent than professionals now believe it to be, although controversy still rages in this area because of the great difficulty in accurately reporting a phenomenon characterized by secrecy and shame. But many of the most egregious cases of group abuse or ritual abuse reported in the 1980s were found to be distortions caused by overzealous investigation. For child professionals, including teachers, child care workers, pediatricians, and therapists, sexual abuse has retreated into a manageable, or at least familiar, place: the investigative and treatment protocols are in place, and the professional hysteria has subsided. This sophistication has not passed over into the public at large, however, and it is unlikely that it will for anyone who lived through the 1980s, when it seemed that new reports of child abuse scandals appeared almost daily in the national press.

The self-esteem movement was another wave of national concern that began with a powerful statement from academicians based upon highly questionable research findings. In 1987, the state of California created the California Task Force to Promote Self-Esteem and Personal and Social Responsibility, thanks to the efforts of Assemblyman John Vasconcellos. The creation of the task force was supported by several academicians from the University of California, including anthropologist Andrew Mecca, who stated that "virtually every social problem we have can be linked to people's lack of self-love: alcohol and drug abuse, teen pregnancy, crime, child abuse, chronic welfare dependency, and poor educational performance." The movement has come and largely gone, but in its day it was extremely popular, spawning several self-esteem curricula that were used nationwide at both the elementary and high school levels. These curricula included inspirational tales about characters who functioned well when they felt good about themselves, like Pumsy the Dragon, and also included the faintly absurd "It's so great to be me" writing assignments and art projects that children brought home from school in the late eighties and early nineties. The self-esteem movement was demolished under the weight of its own excesses, but also by incisive analyses like William Damon's book *Greater Expectations* and John P. Hewitt's *The Myth of Self-Esteem*. Damon and Hewitt went on the counteroffensive, pointing out what every beginning statistics student knows: self-esteem may be correlated with achievement, but that correlation is not necessarily causative. In fact, the direction of causality may be just the reverse, and high self-esteem may be the result of, not the cause of, superior achievement. Whatever self-esteem is, it is probably mitigated by hundreds of factors, so a simple directional prediction would be pretty hard to come by. In any case, as Damon and many others have argued, maybe what we need to be doing to boost our children's self-esteem is asking them to achieve more so they can have something to be proud of, rather than trying to make them feel proud *so that* they will achieve more.

But in my experience, parents' concern for their children's self-esteem has not abated. Like the father who wanted the teacher to make other children laugh at his child's jokes, many parents are terrified about the negative psychological consequences of their children's failures, however trivial. They were alive during the self-esteem craze; they remember hearing how important it is. Self-esteem, we may not remember, was once a relatively specific and measurable psychological construct; now parents use the word as if they were saying "milk" or "air" or any other thing a child so obviously needs.

It remains to be seen what will happen with the current

wave of anxiety regarding school violence. Nothing makes parents worry more than their children's actual physical safety, and the facts of the Columbine incident and other school shootings of the late 1990s are not in dispute. New problems facing parents and schools—including the prediction of violence and mental illness, the eradication of weapons from schools in a culture where weapons are readily available, and, most difficult of all, the limiting of aggression between children—are all being worked out in a context of urgency, which is never the best context for reasoned policy making. But the lessons of the recent past suggest that once the professionals have developed strategies that make the problem more manageable *for professionals* (including protocols for identifying potentially violent children, better resources for referral and treatment of those children, and preventive programs for improving the safety of the school community), the professionals will settle into a more or less routine sophistication about this problem. The worries on the part of the parent community, however, for anyone who was alive in 1999, are far less likely to go away.

The solution to this problem, then, might be simple: people need to pay a lot less attention to the child crisis of the month. But this also begs the question of *why* is it so hard for people to pay less attention to the child crisis of the month. Ignoring hyperbole is not really that hard: in some contexts, people find it easy to ignore media tall tales. When the *Weekly World News* reports the exploits of Bat Boy, the half boy, half bat creature, or reports the latest news about Satan's infiltration of the U.S. government, most people smile and ignore it. Common sense tells us that Bat Boy can't really exist. But common sense tells us that parenting now is really difficult, and that our children are really at risk; the media hyperbole about children could not succeed if it did not resonate with people's widespread, natural, unexamined, so-true-it-doesn't-need-explaining conviction that raising children now is harder than ever.

The conviction that raising children is harder now than it ever was is based upon a set of subconvictions that are heard so often that they are no longer examined. The three subconvictions, the *reasons* given by most parents I know for why raising children is harder today, are that the world is so much more *competitive* today, so much more *unsafe* today, and so much more *confusing* today than it was when we were growing up. These are powerful convictions, and they are held by every parent I know. It is extremely hard to prove or to disprove that the world is actually more competitive, dangerous, and confusing than it was in the past, but the perception of the world is what matters most when parents worry about their children. We can, however, address parental worrying by thinking about the sources of these powerful convictions.

PARENTAL WORRYING AND FAMILY SIZE

Let's begin with a structural reason that might explain why a whole group of people seem more worried than they used to be: they are parents of a small number of children. If it is true—and common sense, as well as decades of psychological research, demonstrates that it is true—that parents of firstborn children are more anxious than other parents, then we would expect that as family size goes down, the average level of parental worrying in the population must necessarily go up. The kind of placidity and blissful nonchalance that characterizes the parenting of younger children in a large family is rapidly becoming a forgotten memory.*

The trend toward smaller families is complicated by divorce rates and "blended" families: many children live in two families at once, and these families are of different sizes. But the overall trends are unmistakable: The U.S. Census Bureau reported in March 2000 that family groups with four or more

---

* As the sixth of seven children, I was one of those children whose older siblings were frequently shocked and annoyed by what I was allowed to get away with. Parents of really large families have truly seen it all, and they worry a lot less—but not until they get to the younger children.

children comprised 17 percent of families in 1970; by 1980, this was down to 8 percent, and in 1990 and 2000 it dropped to 6 percent. Of households with children in the United States, the most common family size was one child (16.2 million families), followed closely by two children (13.9 million families). The numbers drop precipitously after that: households with three and four-or-more children numbered 5.2 million and 2.1 million, respectively. The reasons for this trend are complicated and far beyond the scope of this book; economists usually describe the trend toward smaller families in developed countries as a function of a shift from labor-intensive, agrarian economies to industrial and then technologically based economies, where vast numbers of child farmworkers are not necessary for family prosperity. But whatever the reasons, it is clear that the vast majority of American children are now living with either no siblings or one sibling. Three-child families are now big, and four-child families are enormous.

The explanations for increased parental worrying in small families might best be summarized in two broad categories: reasons derived from evolutionary theory and reasons derived from the lived experience of parenting. The evolutionary theories are the offspring of the pioneering work of evolutionary biologist Robert Trivers, whose 1972 paper defining "parental investment" is one of the landmark papers in what is now called evolutionary psychology. Trivers defined parental investment as "any investment by an individual parent in an individual offspring that increases the offspring's chance of surviving (and hence [the offspring's] reproductive success) at the cost of the parent's ability to invest in other offspring." The motives behind much of human behavior are understood as manifestations of differing parental investment strategies: different species solve the problem in different ways, but the goal of getting as many genes as possible into subsequent generations is the same for all animals, according to evolutionary theory. This theory has been invoked to explain all sorts of human behavior, but it has vast implications for child rearing. Parental investment is a theory of predicting choices animals make, and it is used to explain why, for example, a mother pig or cat will let the runt of a litter starve to death: the parent chooses to invest its finite resources in those offspring which are the most likely to survive and reproduce. Parental investment theory has been used in recent years to explain why birth children are treated better than adoptees, and even to explain attachment to children: children who are seen, somehow, as runts to begin with, and who therefore have low potential for getting more genes into succeeding generations, are said to be more likely to be neglected, or even abused.

Parental investment theory, however, works best in practice if one has a large number of offspring. If we believe that humans really are this coldly calculating (and even if the calculation is happening outside awareness, it's pretty cold), the best strategy for having successful children would be to have a large number of children and to invest more resources, including the resources of time, attention, and education, on the children most likely to succeed. This is the way humans have worked for millennia, and the way many humans still operate. For example, a patient of mine who was born in South Asia struggled to understand American schooling and what he felt to be the radical character of compulsory universal education. In his country, there was no such thing as treatment for things like attention-deficit disorder, because children who could not sit still were not sent to school. It was thought to be a waste of precious resources to try to educate someone whose essential character made him or her unfit for formal education. This is parental investment theory in action: the survival of the fittest child is aided and abetted by parents, who make judgments from the very beginning of life about which of their offspring are the fittest.

Evolutionary psychologists are murky, at best, when trying to explain the current trend toward smaller families. They always have an out, of course: it is never known whether any present behavior is adaptive or maladaptive, and no one can say with certainty whose genes will win out—humans who stick with the time-honored strategy of having many children and investing in the apparent winners, or humans who have fewer children and invest heavily in them no matter what. Obviously, there are more resources to go around for children in smaller families, and modern medicine may be leveling the playing field for the apparent runts. The evolutionary jury is still out, so to speak, on any particular human parental investment strategy.

And since we have several millennia while we wait for the jury to come back in, we have time to speculate about the effects, in terms of parental worrying, about having all our eggs (or genes) in one or two baskets. Evolutionary psychology predicts that getting more of our genes into the next generation is the first principle of human motivation, and all other motivations (like love, justice, and patriotism) are derivatives of this first principle. If we accept this first principle, we might expect that smaller families will necessarily result in higher parental worrying. Seen in this light, overprotection is a no-brainer: abstract and intangible psychological goals like *developing courage,* which are thought to flow from letting children take risks, are meaningless when literal survival of the sole offspring is at stake. If one allows children to take physical risks or to look after themselves in a risky world, and one has six children, one might end up with five courageous, self-directed children, which might be just the thing, evolutionarily speaking. But if one has one child, a parenting style that emphasizes survival and dispenses with developing courage might also be just the thing.

I want to be very clear that in pursuing this line of discussion, I do not imply any moral opprobrium to be laid at the doorstep of parents of small families. I believe that it is common sense, and certainly resonates with our own intuition, that people who have fewer children make different decisions than people who have many children. I do not believe that the wish to have smaller families is evidence of self-indulgence or narcissism or some other contemporary version of being in a state of sin. There are some in our current political climate who sense a moral decline in parents' decisions to have smaller families—that is, people have fewer children because they want to have or spend more money on themselves or their children. House Majority Whip Tom DeLay, for example, made big headlines in 1999 when, in the wake of the Columbine shootings, he argued on the floor of the House of Representatives that "we have sterilized and contracepted our families down to sizes so small that the children we do have are so spoiled with material things that they have come to equate the receiving of the material with love." Most parents I know have small families not in order to spoil the one or two children they do have but because they are daunted by the perceived cost of raising a child and preparing that child to flourish in a competitive world. In other words, most parents describe a parental investment strategy that fits with the facts of the world as they see them, and the strategy they describe is investment in a small number of children precisely because they feel that is best for the children.

*　　*　　*

Abandoning, for the moment, the stylish brutality of evolutionary biology and the somewhat less stylish brutality of contemporary politics, we can understand increased parental worrying in small families in another way, by simply attending to the lived experience of small families. The psychological literature on birth order allows us to think about the effects of living in a culture in which many people are firstborn children. In the census figures from 2000 cited above, all of the only children are by definition also firstborns, and half of the children in two-child families are firstborn children.

Firstborn children are, obviously, born to parents with no experience of parenting. Many parents of larger families joke about "making all the mistakes the first time around," but this old joke contains a profound truth. Parents of firstborn children don't, as a rule, know what they're doing,* and they don't know much about child development. As a result, they tend to overestimate children's malleability. In an extensive 1986 review of research on only children, psychologists Toni Falbo and Denise Polit point out that it has been established for several decades that the transition to parenthood is accompanied by a great deal of anxiety, as would be expected in any situation where the rules are complex and the stakes, apparently, enormous. Published research has shown that first-time parents misjudge the amount of time it takes for children to accomplish developmental milestones: they consistently underestimate how long it takes for a child to be toilet trained, to speak a complete sentence, or to sleep through the night. The parental ignorance that drives these misperceptions is thought to contribute to some of the psychological characteristics shared by oldest *and* only children: they consistently demonstrate more achievement motivation than later-born children. Falbo and Polit suggest that the pushing by first-time parents is not necessarily derived from parents' ambition for the child but derived from a lack of knowledge about developmental milestones, and this pushing to do everything early results in a child's internalization of a lifelong tendency to want to achieve.

Falbo and Polit used, in their review, the statistical technique called meta-analysis, which combines the sizes of statistical effects from a large number of research studies; their review looked at 115 studies on only children, published from the 1920s through the 1980s. Meta-analysis is often used to clarify large-scale trends in behavioral science research, where dozens or hundreds of research studies with differing, and sometimes contradictory, findings make generalization extremely difficult. In their meta-analysis, Falbo and Polit looked at a wide variety

* I make an exception here for parents of firstborn children who have chosen to work with children as a profession. Some of the best new parents I have known are schoolteachers and day care workers.

of outcome measures to see if any of the myths about only children—they are spoiled, they are overanxious, they are neurotic, and so forth—were true. The meta-analysis looked at the achievement, adjustment, character, intelligence, and sociability of only children, and compared only children to children in different family sizes. The results demonstrated that only children were better off than other children in several measured areas: they were more intelligent, demonstrated more achievement motivation as well as measured achievement, and demonstrated better character, on assessments of leadership, autonomy, maturity, cooperativeness, and citizenship. In the areas of sociability and overall emotional adjustment, there were no significant differences between only children and children from larger families. More important for our discussion, Falbo and Polit showed that only children were not statistically different from firstborn children or from children in small families (that is, children in two-child families). The statistical break point seems to come after two children: children in families larger than two were different from children in smaller families, and largely worse off on measures of intelligence, achievement, and character. In terms of developmental outcomes, only children, firstborns, and children in two-child families are all peas in the same pod. That pod is one characterized by high parental worrying, high parental investment, and low competition for the economic and attentional resources of the parents.

These psychological characteristics might be created by the fact that many American children are *accidentally* in small families. Delayed childbearing causes many couples to have only one child, not by plan but by the natural outcome of reduced fertility as mothers age. High rates of divorce also affect these findings: many couples have only one child and then divorce, but they did not initially plan to have only one child (nor did they plan, presumably, to divorce). Research studies in other countries suggest that the effects on a society of having a large number of only children may be less than optimal, but these studies have been largely confined to China, where the one-child policy was adopted in the late 1970s to avoid the widespread famine that was projected to accompany unchecked population growth. Chinese research on the psychological effects on children and families of the one-child policy is, in general, less optimistic than similar research in the United States: Chinese only children are, like U.S. only children, more intelligent but are more likely than their U.S. counterparts to be described as fussy, willful, and uncooperative. The reasons for this are unclear, but researchers suggest that these differences might be due to a crucial difference between these two populations: in China, parents know from birth that their one child will be their only child; in the United States, children are more likely to end up as only children, but this is not known from day one. American parents may be overinvested, or ignorant about what children are really like, but they might not be as consistently desperate about their children's fates as their Chinese counterparts.

❊   ❊   ❊

It makes sense that people who are raising children for the first time are more worried about it because of a lack of experience, and it makes sense that as the proportion of families with one or two children goes up, the proportion of worried parents will also go up. But it is not only new parents' lack of experience with raising children that makes them worried. There is also the experience of children's temperament—or, one might say, the *respect* for children's inborn temperament—which is gained only after exposure to larger numbers of children that one has known since birth.

The issue of children's temperament is profound, in a historical sense (we will return to this issue in Chapter 2). At this juncture, we can simply state that people with greater experience with children, especially their own children, have a deeper understanding of the fact that children come with a great deal of personality already present. This has been dramatically demonstrated by the studies of twins separated at birth that have been conducted for thirty years by behavioral geneticist David Lykken at the University of Minnesota: tastes in clothes, tastes in food, tastes in spouses, personal habits, physical gestures, and intellectual and artistic passions are all highly correlated in identical twins, even those raised in completely separate environments. But parents of several children don't need to read research to know that this is true. Parents of several children have an opportunity to observe differences in inborn temperament or character firsthand, and as a result, they are always less invested in trying to change children into something else.

As a knowledge problem, it makes sense that parents might assume, of their own first child, that "all kids are like that." Indeed, one of the things parents of first children very frequently say to a therapist is, "I thought all kids were like that—until I had a second kid." But those who don't have the second kid, and those who have not yet had the second kid, are still making the logical but erroneous assumption that their only child, with his or her unique character, is the standard model.

PIGS AND PONIES

As family sizes drift down, we as a society become a group of parents who were raised in larger families raising children in smaller families. Biologically, this is an odd idea; if we were animals, it would be like being born into a large litter of pigs but giving birth to offspring that are born in ones or twos, like ponies. What knowledge would we bring to the task that might be irrelevant, or just plain wrong?

In thinking about these structural issues, we have already considered the effects of raising mostly a group of only or firstborn children: the heightened worries that attend this particular experience are simply magnified as the proportion of small families in the general population goes up. But there is also the psychological effect of having been raised in larger families, and raising children without that experience. What does it mean to have the experience we have had, and to project it, psychologically, onto our children?

In general, children in larger families have to be more competitive for the precious resources of parental time and attention. To the degree that this sense of competition is internalized, we can assume that children raised in somewhat larger families will bring with them, into their adult lives, a sense that competition is a sometimes unpleasant but undeniable fact of human existence. *But our children's lives are not like that.* As generations of parents projecting our own experience onto our children—that is, using our own experience to imagine what their experience must be like—we make a big mistake if we think their lives are as competitive as ours were. "The world is more competitive today" may be our way of saying, "The world was very competitive for me, so I imagine it will also be for my child." But what if it's not? Most of our children have resources available to them that we did not, precisely because they come from smaller families. If attention from adults is a resource that is valuable (and it is) and something worth competing for (which children do), their experience will be very different from our own. There will always be individuals whose experience runs the other way—people who grew up in small families and are raising large families. But these individuals are a very small minority of the current population. For the most part we are, whether we like it or not, a bunch of pigs raising our own little ponies. It's an absurd image, but then again, it is absurd to try to use our knowledge of being a child in a large family to raise a child now. Our children's world is a different world, but technological change, the usual culprit here, is not the only contributor to this difference.

Luckily, there are many things that are the same from one generation to the next. Technology can feel like the villain, making the world of our children incomprehensible to us. It can also be seen as the hero: so much of human life has been vastly improved with technological advances that we might feel that parental decision making can be improved with more scientific, technology-driven knowledge. It might make things better, and it might make things worse. But we do not need technology to know the principles of good parenting. Regardless of the size of any particular family, we know what good parents do, and there is plenty of knowledge already on the books to demonstrate what good parenting is all about. Part of the task of reducing parental worrying is reducing the clutter of information to the essential principles, the things good parents do and have been doing for a very, very long time.

Two

DR. SCHREBER
AND MRS. JELLYBY:
THE MYTH OF SCIENTIFIC
PARENTING

Leslie has a real problem, but she doesn't know it.* She is a mother of two children, aged thirteen and ten, and she is trying hard to be the best parent she can be. Leslie's younger daughter complains to me, privately, that her mom is never available to do anything in the evening: she is too busy to help with homework, she is too busy to play a game or watch TV; she is just too busy. Her daughter complains bitterly about the loss of her mother's attention. But, asks the therapist, what is she so busy doing? She is sitting in front of the computer, scouting out parenting tips from Web sites, chat rooms, and problem-specific sites dedicated to distributing the latest research findings on child development and parenting.

Leslie is an educated person, and she may have read Charles Dickens's *Bleak House,* which contains a description of

---

* Throughout this book, real names have been changed and identifying information omitted.

the remarkable Mrs. Jellyby, a Victorian do-gooder who spends all her time reading, writing, and preaching about the plight of poor children in Africa, while her own children are pitiably ignored. The character type is not new, although Leslie gives this role a particularly modern twist. She may, like Mrs. Jellyby, suffer from a wish to avoid the complexities of real human interaction, but for the moment let's give Leslie credit for being a good mother. She is doing what she thinks she needs to do. In the face of a confusing situation, she is doing what any educated and practical citizen would do. She is gathering more data to find out how to do things right before she does them wrong—in the words of the old proverb, she believes one should "measure twice, cut once." She is a devotee of scientific parenting.

Scientific parenting is not new, either; indeed, it is at least as old as behavioral science. At around the same time Dickens was inventing Mrs. Jellyby, a German physician named Daniel Gottlieb Moritz Schreber was writing a series of extremely popular parenting manuals, which advised forward-looking parents of the day on how to raise disciplined, morally good children. The science of the day, as described by Dr. Schreber, suggested that children needed to be broken of their natural laziness and moral turpitude. Schreber designed a number of mechanical devices for correcting children's posture, and he also suggested a series of disciplinary techniques meant to eradicate not only children's outward, or behavioral, rebelliousness but even their interior, mental rebelliousness. His books were devoured throughout the German-speaking world in the middle of the nineteenth century.

Dr. Schreber was famous in his day, and he was the father of a famous son: his son, Dr. Daniel Paul Schreber, was the author of the sensational book *Memories of My Nervous Illness*. In the book, Schreber the son describes his (plainly delusional) torment at the hands of a sadistic and capricious God, who had chosen the author to be his sexual partner in founding a new, superior version of the human race. Schreber the son became even more famous when he became the subject of one of Sigmund Freud's book-length case histories, *Psychoanalytic Notes on an Autobiographical Account of a Case of Paranoia (Dementia Paranoides)*. Although he was also a brilliant jurist, Schreber the son is best remembered today for being a famous madman.

In reading the advice given out by the elder Schreber now, one is struck by the sadistic nature of the disciplinary tools suggested. But one is also struck by the moral instruction, the sermonizing, being cast in the language of science: Schreber rests his authority not on God, but on the findings of contemporary medical science. If this disjunction seems crude by modern standards, it is because behavioral pediatric science was then in its infancy. Schreber calls himself a scientist, but his recommendations, which may have sprung from moral principles, personal idiosyncrasies, or his own mental illness, are unconvincing because there is little scientific proof to back them up.

Fast-forward a century or more. It is 1990, the beginning of what the American Psychological Association dubbed the Decade of the Brain, and research on brain processes was exploding, thanks to innovations in technology that allow for sophisticated, real-time pictures of the living human brain at work. In this decade, research on brain development was also exploding: we learned an astonishing amount about how and when larger structures in the brain develop and about the chemistry of neurotransmitters and cortical steroids that affect brain development. The new science of the brain is breathtaking, but we are left with a nagging similarity to the parenting manuals of the Victorian age: the link between the new science and the practical application thereof is tenuous at best. At its worst, today's science is a cover for moralizing, or pursuing a political or ethical agenda that has nothing to do with science at all.

Let's look at a contemporary example. In late 2000, *News-*

week magazine brought out a special issue devoted to "Your Child: Birth to Three." In the lead article, "21st Century Babies," Barbara Kantrowitz wrote:

> If you're a new parent, your baby had the good fortune to be born at a truly remarkable moment in human history, when science has given us extraordinary new tools for understanding what kids need to thrive physically, emotionally and intellectually. . . . At the dawn of the 21st century, we no longer have to guess about the best way to raise a child. That wasn't the case for most of the last hundred years, as parenting theories swung back and forth between permissive and strict without much basis in science. . . . Thanks to the Internet, these breakthroughs are no longer lost in the pages of some obscure scientific journal. There are literally hundreds of thousands of child-rearing Web sites—some dispensing information and others forming virtual park benches so parents continents apart can share their common joys and growing pains.

It's no wonder Leslie is so busy at that computer. She needs to catch up on all the latest scientific research, which will tell her, once and for all, the really scientific way to raise her children. The promise is that we are at long last able to go beyond opinion to fact. The problem is that it still won't work. Scientific parenting is still a myth.

The fascinating data provided by PET scans and sophisticated neurotransmitter studies are wonderful to behold. They provide a window into what is happening, *at a neurophysiological level,* in the brains of developing children. This data is invaluable in terms of establishing baselines in the study of abnormal development: the baseline studies of normal brains can then be used to understand when a brain is abnormal. Beyond that, we are faced with another kind of problem. Does this data tell us anything new or different about how to be a good parent?

The data demonstrate beyond the shadow of a doubt that stimulation, whether it is tactile, visual, or auditory, has some neurophysiological correlates. When a developing nervous system is stimulated, it changes in ways that an unstimulated nervous system does not. This finding, while dramatically depicted in recent human brain research, is also not particularly new. Neuroscience research on nonhuman animals demonstrated more than twenty years ago that rats raised in spatial environments rich in stimulation showed demonstrable changes in the weight of brain structures as well as increased complexity of structure in particular cells in the central nervous system. This research, conducted by W. T. Greenough and others, was published in the early seventies, and the findings were used to justify everything from the necessity for early education, including Head Start, to the design of particular child care environments. Many busy early-childhood spaces of those days were designed to be a human analogue of the rich environments that made Greenough's rat brains so heavy and complex. But as many critics of the day pointed out, moving from the rat research to the design of particular early-childhood environments was probably overextending the limits of the sound scientific findings.

Today's brain research goes further in the direction of demonstrating the effects of stimulation on humans. Practically speaking, one could argue that the best recommendation to come out of the new brain research is that neglect is bad for children; it is not only bad for children's emotional life, but also bad, apparently, for their neurophysiological life. So the best, safest, most clear recommendation here would be: don't neglect your children. Don't leave them in their cribs for hours at a time with nothing to look at. Do talk to them. Don't leave them alone for days on end. Do touch them, wash them, and play with them. Do something with them.

These recommendations are not as trivial as they seem. For

children of depressed parents or impoverished parents, these are real issues: parents who are depressed or severely limited by poverty or social isolation are at serious risk for understimulating their children. But even the reported neurological insults in populations of neglected children (for example, Romanian orphans) have yet to be documented with a reasonable degree of scientific certainty, because these children are also exposed to so many risk factors for brain damage, like poor prenatal nutrition, current malnutrition, and exposure to environmental toxins. So if the effect of *severe* pathological neglect on developing brains is still hard to sort out, one would expect that the effects of variable, but essentially normal, parenting practices would be exceedingly difficult to find. Where does this leave us in the search for practical implications of the new brain research for ordinary parents?

Is there a way to argue, based upon the current research, that certain types of stimulation are better than others? Is it better, for example, to have a child in preschool, where there is a range of activities with other adults and children, like playing with blocks, talking about colors, singing, and hearing books read aloud? Or is it better for a child to be with a parent or caregiver all day, participating in a range of activities, including shopping, going along while the adult cooks or exercises, talking with an adult about the world, singing, and hearing her read books aloud? At this level of specificity, the new brain research dictates nothing. As long as a child is being stimulated, there is no evidence to recommend anything more particular about the type of stimulation he or she should receive.

In the same issue of *Newsweek* that trumpets the new brain research as the final answer to parenting issues, numerous child development experts and neuroscientists are consulted about the implications of the new research. For example, developmental psychologist Andrew Meltzoff notes that babies learn through "mini-experiments with pots and pans, and by playing peekaboo and other everyday games." *Newsweek* also quotes a new report from the National Academy of Sciences, called

"The Science of Early Childhood Development," as follows: "Given the drive of young children to master their world . . . the full range of early childhood competencies can be achieved in typical, everyday environments. A cabinet with pots and pans . . . seems to serve the same purpose as a fancy, 'made for baby' musical instrument." A skeptical consumer might notice, at this point, the radical disjunction between the sophistication of the new brain research and the simplicity of the recommendations that flow from it: essentially, let your child play with pots and pans.

In the professional community, scientists involved with brain development research are a careful lot, and their concern about the hyping of the new brain research is everywhere. For example, the public information campaign in 1997 called "I Am Your Child" included nationwide television specials, a White House conference on early-childhood development, and a popular Web site bearing the I Am Your Child name; the central focus of this information campaign was the scientific necessity of early stimulation for healthy brain development. In a review of this campaign in 2001, psychologists Ross Thompson and Charles Nelson, writing in the *American Psychologist*, appreciated that the I Am Your Child campaign stimulated a burst of public investment in early-childhood programs. However, Thompson and Nelson go on to state,

> media accounts have also tended to exaggerate how much is actually known about the developing brain, overinterpreting current scientific knowledge and overpromising its applications while also unduly narrowing public understanding of the range of important influences on brain development. . . . The concern is not simply that the scientific picture is far more complex than its representation in the media. . . . More important, however, is that valuable public interest in early childhood may evaporate as quickly as it has emerged if parents, practitioners, and policymakers conclude that

they were misled about how they could contribute to optimizing early development, especially if simplified interpretations and applications of research on early brain development do not yield outcomes for enhanced intellectual and socioemotional growth.

Clearly, these scientists, and many others like them, are concerned about being the twenty-first-century versions of Drs. Klaus and Kennell: they do not want the new research to be oversold and then rejected when the miraculous new information does not produce miraculous results.

Since the current science-based brain research really doesn't yield specific, science-based recommendations, one sees, by necessity, the return of the subtle ideological creep. It is harder to discern than in old Dr. Schreber's moralizing pronouncements, but it is still there. If the new research really does not yet dictate clear prescriptions (Thompson and Nelson go so far as to say that the study of human brain development is "still in its infancy"), then the premature practical applications of this research must be based upon something else. And in most cases, it is based upon old-fashioned *philosophies* of child rearing: just the things that the new research is supposed to consign to oblivion.

This difficulty highlights the most profound tension in the field of parenting today. Whether we like it or not, and many of us don't, values continue to creep into what is supposed to be a scientific enterprise. Science is, after all, supposed to be objective: it is value-neutral. The wish expressed by so many parents I know (and I know because they ask me all the time) is that new research, the newest and most high-tech research, will settle these questions once and for all. It is, simply, the wish that science will come to the rescue and settle the questions about values that make many parents uneasy—and then parents won't have to make value decisions themselves.

Here's a brief example. New research, using the sophisticated tools of modern medicine, has recently focused on the phenomenon of sleep deprivation and the rhythms of the sleep-wake cycle in adolescents. Dr. Mary Carskadon of Brown University has been in the forefront of this research, and her work has been widely reported in the public press, in a special series of articles called "Inside the Teen Brain" in *U.S. News & World Report* in 1999, and in a PBS *Frontline* special of the same name that aired early in 2002. Carskadon's research documents that many contemporary adolescents are sleep-deprived: many teens are going to school without having had enough sleep, so much so that they appear, on medical assessment, to be similar to adult narcoleptics. Carskadon and her associates have also documented a relationship between sleep and grades: kids who get more sleep tend to get higher grades on average than kids who get less sleep.

These findings are unequivocal: the science of sleep research has documented the phenomenon of teen sleep deprivation very convincingly. But what is to be done about this problem? The new research tells us that teens need more sleep. Okay, now what?

One of the outcomes of Carskadon's research has been a movement to change the start times of schools so that teenagers start their school day an hour or so later. This movement is a direct outcome of the new sleep research and it cites that research as a primary motivation for the later-start-times recommendation. Many schools in Minnesota have already implemented this change in social policy, and there have been some reported increases in school attendance and school grades for teenagers who start school an hour later than they used to.

The old-fashioned parent might say at this point, "Why can't they just go to bed earlier?" Indeed, that is what many parents and adults do say, in response to the suggestions for later school start times for high school students. For Carskadon, this is a simplistic response to a complicated question. Her research demonstrates that there may be a period of activation in teenagers' sleep-wake cycles that makes it more difficult to fall asleep between the hours of ten and twelve at night. But she also points out that children's lives are complicated. Many of them work late hours in the evening, and many of them have computers and televisions and telephones in their rooms, which offer endless distractions. These distractions, which may be seen as an unchangeable feature of adolescent culture, make it even more difficult for adolescents to go to sleep earlier, in order to get the nine hours of sleep they need each night.

Case closed, right? Science says they can't go to sleep earlier in the evening, therefore we must change school start times. But a closer look at these arguments points out the values that creep into arguments that are supposedly settled by value-free scientific research.

First of all, there is the value of *We need to sacrifice for them.* Going to sleep earlier in the evening is hard for them, so we need to change our schedules. We need to rearrange our child care, workdays, family mealtimes, and every other feature of adult life (and if families have younger children with earlier start times and older children with later start times, this can be a real nightmare) because it is hard for them to go to sleep. The implicit value that underlies all parenting—self-sacrifice—is put into operation once again here: we need to make our lives harder rather than ask them to make their lives harder.

One way we could ask them to make their lives harder is to turn off the computer, television, and phones so that, even though they may be having a biological window of wakefulness to overcome, they have a reasonable chance of overcoming it. Carskadon's research does not, after all, demonstrate that it is *impossible* for teens to fall asleep between 10 and 12 P.M.; it is just more difficult. If it is a little more difficult for them to fall asleep during those hours, we could ask them to make it a little easier by shutting down the electronic playground. But the next unspoken value, *Childhood is a time for fun,* creeps in and prevents many parents from making this perfectly reasonable request. Many parents would automatically upend their lives in the morning rather than take away their children's fun in the evening.

And even if we do somehow summon the courage to turn off the toys, and a child still (for biological reasons, as Carskadon's work suggests) has trouble falling asleep at a reasonable hour, what then? Then the value of *We can't ask them to do something that is (biologically) hard for them to do* comes in. If it is difficult for them to do, if they are not yet ready, biologically, to fall asleep at a reasonable hour, then we can't ask it of them . . . can we?

It might sound scientific to assume that we cannot ask of people what they cannot (physically) do, but in fact, this is a value statement as well. To wait until a child's biological capacity to perform an action is fully developed before expecting competent performance is a philosophy at one end of a spectrum, and an extreme end at that. In fact, we expect children to do what they cannot (yet) do all the time: if we didn't, there would be no development.

An example is reading, a skill that does not develop at all naturally: unlike speaking, people need to be taught to read. And most people, except in extreme educational systems, begin to teach reading while a child is still developing the mental hardware needed to read. In more extreme or dogmatic schools (as, for example, those established according to principles set forth by Rudolf Steiner), children wait until they are *all* known to be anatomically ready to read before they begin learning to read (thus the famous Steiner dictum that one does not begin learning to read until one's adult teeth come in). But this is an extreme, and it is a value-driven system. There is no research that actually suggests that the strategy of waiting until children are anatomically completely ready to read produces superior readers.

The entire process of teaching—and parenting, as we shall see—is the process of asking people to learn to do what they cannot yet do. It is also the process of psychotherapy, and, one would argue, it is a value that informs almost all of mental health treatment. If, for example, we assume that people with mental illnesses are biologically incapable of doing certain things, and we do not then ask them to do these things, this is a value judgment, not a recommendation from the world of value-neutral science.* So, when we approach adolescents with demands for going to sleep at a reasonable hour, we can be aware that, because of their immature neurological status, this is harder for them than it is for us; and *we can ask them to do it anyway.* How much we ask of them, and how we ask it of them, is still a parenting decision that we must make, and abdicating this hard decision-making to scientists is not going to make it any easier.

Carskadon herself, being a careful scientist, knows this. She very carefully does not personally advocate later start times for adolescents in school. She advocates, based upon her research, more sleep for adolescents, a good, careful recommendation that does not go beyond the data. She also advocates better education about sleep and sleep deprivation, so that parents and teenagers know the risks and understand that they are not omnipotent when it comes to the demands of the body. But this has not stopped passionate advocates for later start times from using her research to argue forcefully that this controversial change in public policy *must* be adopted.

The foregoing is not meant to imply that modern medical and neuroscience research is not wonderful. It is wonderful, in the way that all knowledge is wonderful, even if the uses for it are not immediately apparent. But the translation of new research in neuroscience or brain development into parenting practice and public policy has to be made with caution, and the scientists doing this research will be the first ones to tell us that. After all, many of the new findings about brain development

---

* As one of my old and dear teachers, a Southern gentleman and a therapist of great renown for seriously disturbed people, once said, "Mental illness is no excuse for bad manners." Asking people to develop beyond and despite their biological limitations, it could be argued, is much more humane than not asking them to do so.

are findings about neurological correlates of observed behavior: we already know, for example, that many adolescents are impulsive, and the finding that this impulsivity has a neurological substrate is not particularly surprising, since all human behavior has a neurological substrate. But the danger now is the same as it has been for the last two hundred years: that hidden or unspoken values creep into parenting recommendations under the cloak of value-free science.

INFORMATION OVERLOAD AND PARENTAL ANXIETY

So one problem with depending upon new scientific findings is that it doesn't really substitute for making parenting choices based upon values. If we assume that it will, we are fooling ourselves, and pushing scientists into a role of premature recommenders, a role that many of the most reputable scientists are very unwilling to fill. But there is another reason why doing our homework, or trying to solve parenting problems by applying an engineering solution, is bound to contribute to increased parental worrying. That other problem is information overload.

Information overload confronts many Americans in many walks of life. As some have argued, information overload and the anxiety that accompanies it are a direct result of the changes in Americans' attitude toward expertise and paternalism that have been brought about in the last several decades. The slow demise of the paternalistic expert has been most visible in the world of medicine, and this demise has only been speeded up by the development of the Internet and the increased availability of medical information to the general public. People with common physical conditions like menopause and common illnesses like cancer can be inundated with information and conflicting recommendations simply by turning on the computer: the culture does not, in these instances, speak with one voice.

Even when the information is not about a life-or-death concern, too much information may be a major contributor to changes in the quality of contemporary life. Some social psychologists have recently begun referring to the "tyranny of choice." The phrase refers to the increased anxiety and depression experienced by Americans having too much information, and too many choices to make, about everything. For example, a series of studies by social psychologists Sheena Iyengar and Mark Lepper demonstrated this tyranny of choice simply and elegantly: consumers were forced to choose what they might buy from a large array (thirty or more) versus a small array (six) of products, including gourmet jams and chocolates. In each case, consumers were more likely to make a purchase, and were more likely to be happy with their purchase, when there was a smaller number of choices. A larger number of choices had the effect of paralyzing consumers and making them less happy about the choice they eventually did make. In their research, Iyengar and Lepper noted that, when asked, consumers expressed the desire to have more choices, but in each case, the larger number of choices made them less happy in the long run with the choices they did actually make.

This phenomenon is certainly familiar to me as a child development expert who is often asked for advice. I am frequently asked to recommend a course of action to parents, and in talking with them, I find that they have already read several books and articles and consulted several Web sites that may also make a recommendation. The feeling I encounter is one of frustration: in a decision situation in which the outcome seems crucial, there seems to be no way to find one single answer. Many opinions are offered, and many of them are competing or diametrically opposed. A brief look at parenting chat rooms, or parent-to-parent advice-sharing sites on the Internet, also confirms the observation that parents are overloaded with information: many of these sites have a fair amount of expert-trashing as a primary feature of the discussion. Since experts can't agree, parents turn to other parents on these sites for the ultimate in good advice. It is this confusion of tongues, in fact, that sends so many parents searching for new scientific findings to settle the confusion once and for all. Unfortunately, as we have seen, science can't do this yet, and it may never be able to settle questions of value.

But that doesn't mean we are totally in the dark. We already know, from millennia of experience, and common sense, and decades' worth of good observational parenting research, that there are general principles of good parenting upon which we might all agree. If we know the big principles, we can always test a particular parenting decision to see if it fits into the big picture these principles prescribe. These broad principles of what we already know about good parenting can be summed up in three terms: *moderate firmness, empathy,* and *goodness of fit.*

PARENTING WITH MODERATION

Thinking broadly, the task of parenting involves physical care— providing food, shelter, and protection from predators. Beyond that, it is mostly about a protracted negotiation between the needs of an individual child and the needs of the society in which he or she lives. The family stands in for society for a while; we can think of the primary caregiver as the first in a long line of others (with their own needs) with whom an infant must negotiate.

The issue of infant feeding is a prime example. Should babies be fed on demand, whenever they cry and appear to be hungry? Or should they be fed on a schedule? The realities of how to determine this are messy, but the issue is clear: how much of this activity is going to be determined by the infant's need to be gratified when she feels the need to be gratified, and how much of this activity is going to be determined by the caregiver's need to attend to all the other things a caregiver needs to do?* In a broad philosophical sense, the task of parenting is, simply, managing that negotiation over and over. How much do you do for, give, or satisfy what your kid needs, and how much do you discipline, deprive, socialize, take from, or inspire him, to be a part of the social whole? That's the whole ball game.

Intuition tells us, and everyday life informs us, that any extreme position in this negotiation is not a good idea. We know it is not a good thing to be totally selfish, and we also know that it is not a good thing to be totally selfless. Where one sets the balance in between these two poles involves a constant struggle between individual need and community needs; in that sense, it has the character of a political struggle. It is not for nothing that philosophers have drawn parallels between the family and the state. But ancient philosophers also told us what we intuit must be true of good parenting: that the way of virtue is the way of moderation.

In theory, development experts have extolled the virtues of moderation for a long time. For Freud, the idea of moderation came out of the dynamic balance of conflict between the opposing forces of instinct and civilization: the forces of instinct, located in the body, are always demanding gratification, and the forces of civilization are always demanding repression. Human lives are profitably, or tragically, lived between these two forces, neither of which can be overcome.** These themes are taken up again in, for example, the work of Erik Erikson, who consis-

---

* One could argue here that the infant *needs* to be regularized as soon as possible, and so scheduled feeding is really a response to what the infant needs. In fact, the only reason the infant needs that to be regularized is to internalize, earlier rather than later, the necessity of attending to the needs of others.

** Freud's error, some have argued, was his inability to see how fragile the forces of civilization really are. The dynamic balance he envisioned must necessarily be rethought in a society, like our own, in which the weight of repression is so much lighter than it was in his time.

tently argued for the middle road as the way of psychological health. Erikson argued in *Childhood and Society* that fixation, or the tendency of an individual to get stuck in immature gratifications, was the result of *either not enough or too much* gratification at a particular stage: one could develop an oral character by being orally frustrated (weaned too early) or by being orally overgratified (weaned too late). The optimum strategy was to find the right dynamic balance between the poles of frustration and gratification.

The principle of moderation, affirmed by classical philosophy and enshrined in psychoanalytic theory, has also been demonstrated elegantly over several decades of nitty-gritty observational parenting research. The best exemplar of this research—indeed, some of the best parenting research ever conducted—has been done over the years by Diana Baumrind, a developmental psychologist with more than four decades of parenting research to her credit. Baumrind has continued to demonstrate, and to argue for, the principle of moderation as an effective parenting strategy in both specific and general parenting contexts.

Baumrind's original research was an observational study of children's behavior in a preschool setting coupled with observations of parents' behaviors in the home. She described three types of parenting styles: *authoritarian* parenting, characterized by demands for obedience, as well as punishment when children fail to measure up; *authoritative* parenting, characterized by nonpunitive firmness in a context of explaining principles of parental decisions and listening to children's points of view; and *permissive* parenting, characterized by high levels of child decision making and low levels of parental limit setting. In her observations in preschools, Baumrind and her associates found that children of authoritarian parents were somewhat fearful, socially incompetent, and lacking in curiosity and spontaneity; and not surprisingly, they looked to authorities for guidance and control. Children of authoritative parents were found to be self-controlled, accepting of limits and rules, relatively independent, but also content with rules and structure. Children of permissive parents were less mature than other children, more impulsive, and had more difficulty controlling their behavior in general than the children in either of the other groups. These differences have been demonstrated in populations of high school students as well: children of authoritative parents seem to be the most successful, both academically and socially, of the three groups.

Baumrind's research suggests that there is some optimum middle ground between the extremes of control and permissiveness that not only makes good intuitive sense but also produces healthy children. Although the framework seems incontrovertible, Baumrind herself has managed to generate heat, and light, by sticking to the principle of moderation and rejecting any calls for parenting practices that might be considered extremes. In the summer of 2001, for example, Baumrind made a stir at the annual meeting of the American Psychological Association by presenting her findings and opinions regarding the use of corporal punishment. She argued that corporal punishment is not always bad: in the context of an authoritative parenting style, in which limits are firm and reasons explained, corporal punishment is not an absolute evil. Baumrind's critics, and there are many, have argued for years that corporal punishment is never justified, because it is child abuse in principle as well as being an ineffective parenting strategy. But in an extremely comprehensive look at what parents did with their children and how the children turned out, Baumrind and her colleagues found that moderate amounts of corporal punishment were not associated with any indicators of bad adjustment. There was simply no evidence of any kind in her data base that a little spanking causes any long-term harm to children.

THE ROLE OF EMPATHY
IN GOOD PARENTING

In looking at the descriptions of Baumrind's authoritative parents, one behavior that stands out is *listening*. Parents in this capsule description do not always agree with children, but they make an effort to listen to their child's point of view. In other words, they are big on empathy. The psychological activities subsumed under the heading of empathy are complex, but they have sometimes been described as having a cognitive component (the intellectual ability to understand the point of view of an other) and an affective, or feeling, component (the ability and the wish to understand how another feels).

Parenting research on empathy demonstrates that it is a quality that is most often observed in its absence. When one looks at research on bad outcomes in adulthood, unempathic parenting is very frequently described as a contributing factor. For example, Drew Westen and his colleagues at Boston University have described the role of unempathic parenting in the development of personality disorders in adulthood, a finding echoed by the eminent therapist of personality-disordered people, Marsha Linehan. Unempathic parenting is implicated in parenting research on adolescents with conduct disorders and adolescents who are already juvenile offenders. A lack of empathy is also a characteristic of many parents who are at risk for child abuse: for example, middle-adolescent teenagers who are parents are known to be at a higher risk of abusing their children. One reason for this is the finding that middle adolescents are, for good developmental reasons, still embroiled in their own developmental needs and are not particularly sensitive to, or even aware of, the quite different developmental needs of their children.

It makes good intuitive sense, as well, that empathy is a characteristic of good parenting. Empathy is, in one important sense, an ability and a willingness to gather information about the other, especially the particular inner life of the other. Empathy might not be so important if every child were exactly the same: one would not need to gather data about the inner life of the child from that child in particular. But as recent research has amply demonstrated, all children are not the same, and the individual, inborn temperamental character of a child is a crucial determinant of his or her behavior and development. As I discussed in Chapter 1, one reason why parents today are much more anxious about their children is that they have fewer children, and therefore they have less lived experience of inborn differences between children. Empathy is the tool that parents have to notice those differences. To know whom you are dealing with, you have to work to get to know them, inside and outside, without assuming that you know them ahead of time. An outgoing parent of an extremely shy child, for example, is going to need empathy, because no amount of principle-driven parenting knowledge is going to prepare for the experience of parenting a child who is frequently in so much pain.

Empathy is also a guarantee against unnecessary parental projection. One of the things that drives children crazy (and here I am referring to real clinical dysfunction) is an excess of projection: parents who assume that their children are identical to themselves, and therefore need and want the identical things. A certain amount of projection is inevitable in parenting—"I know what I was like at that age" is always a good exercise—but it is usually wrong to figure that the best way to know your child is to assume that he or she is just like you in every particular. In my own clinical work, this kind of breakdown is most evident in children of divorce: parents who have strong negative feelings toward their ex-spouse frequently make the mistake of assuming that their children have the same experience. "If he was destructive to me, he must be destructive to her" is a conclusion imposed from without, but it is not empathic. Very frequently the hardest thing about a divorce is to allow your beloved child to have a relationship with someone who has acted or felt personally destructive; it is impossible to imagine, for some people, that a husband or wife who would destroy a spouse or a marriage would not also destroy a child in the same way. But they often don't. The child's independent emotional experience of the (hated) ex-spouse is almost impossible to imagine, but that act of imagination is then that much more necessary.

It is also important to note, following Baumrind's work, that empathy is not synonymous with permissiveness. Listening to a child and trying to understand his or her point of view is not the same as caving in. I frequently use the following vignette, from my observation in an excellent nursery school setting, as an example of empathy in action: A child is playing outside on the playground on one of the first beautiful days of spring. The teacher rings the bell signaling it is time to go inside. The child says, "I don't want to go in; it's so nice outside." And the teacher replies, with real warmth and regret in her voice, "I know how hard it is to go inside on such a beautiful day. But it's time to go in, so get in line." And of course the child complies. It might be obvious to anyone who saw or read *Mary Poppins* that "a spoonful of sugar helps the medicine go down." But it is a little more emotionally complicated, and wonderfully effective, to be empathic and to set limits at the same time.

GOODNESS OF FIT

The patroness of the concept of goodness of fit was Stella Chess, a distinguished psychiatrist who for decades was, with her colleague Alexander Thomas, the lead researcher at the New York Longitudinal Study. Chess started the NYLS to demonstrate what she knew from her years as a practicing physician: that all babies are different, right from birth. The NYLS began in the 1950s, in an era when parents, especially mothers, were thought to be the cause of most forms of mental illness. The example Chess always used was the developmental-historical theory of autism, which suggested that even an extreme childhood emotional disorder like autism could be traced to inadequate mothering: the mothers of autistic children were described as cold, aloof, and robotic in their care-giving, which, in turn, produced cold, aloof, robotic children. Chess set out to prove, using the best research methods available to her at the time, that children all come with an inborn temperament, and therefore that not all childhood emotional disturbance could be laid at the door of inadequate parenting. To demonstrate this, she collected systematic observations of infant behavior when her research subjects were just a few weeks old, and then followed them for several decades. What she showed was that there were certain temperamental characteristics that persisted throughout a child's childhood, and well into adulthood. These temperamental differences were observed in several different behavioral contexts and by several different observers (parents first, and later teachers and the research subjects themselves).

What Chess described was three different temperamental clusters: the *easy* child, the *difficult* child, and the *slow-to-warm-up* child. Easy children (about 40 percent of the original NYLS sample) earned this label because they were relatively regular in terms of their needs and moods, relatively open to new experience, and relatively calm or happy most of the time. Difficult children (about 10 percent of the NYLS sample) were irregular, and therefore not easy to get on a schedule, sensitive to minute changes in environmental stimuli, and frequently irritable in response to the ordinary frustrations of everyday life. Slow-to-warm-up children (about 15 percent) were initially avoidant or wary of the new, or fearful of novel stimuli, but they did, with time, warm up to a new situation and adapt with relative comfort.

Chess and Thomas's research has been criticized for its methodological flaws, which may have overestimated temperamental consistency. More recent researchers have shown that temperamental consistency itself is something that some people have more of than others. The issue of temperamental consistency turns out to be sort of a projective test: the correlations in temperament research are never perfect. The correlations between a child's behavior at time one and time two can range from "modest" to "robust," but the consistency, and therefore the role of inborn factors such as temperament, is in the eye of the beholder.

Despite these methodological concerns, Chess and Thomas's major contribution was rhetorical. They clearly and powerfully refuted the concept of the generic baby or child, and thus put to rest the concept of generic parenting advice. Their recommendations to parents were clearly articulated under the concept of goodness of fit, by which they meant an ongoing assessment of the interaction between a child's temperament and the environmental demands placed upon that child. Demands for scheduled feeding or sleeping, for example, are easily accomplished with an easy baby, but a difficult baby needs more accommodation because he or she is temperamentally unready for the same kind of scheduling. These concepts are so familiar to us now, in an era of parenting books about the difficult child, or the anxious child, or the shy child, that we may forget that it was not too long ago that the concept of a dynamic interaction between parenting style and temperamental style was an idea that needed to be fought for in the face of opposition from the scientific community of the day.

Most important for our discussion, however, is the notion set forth by Chess and Thomas that the best way to raise a child is to create a good fit between a child's temperament and the demands of the environment, *but this fit cannot, and should not, be perfect.* Chess and Thomas recommended that a child with a difficult temperament should not be bullied by demands he or she cannot meet, but they also argued passionately that a child's difficult temperament should not rule a family. Compassionate parenting was never thought to be synonymous with permissiveness. Children need firm guidelines and clear demands, according to these pioneers, and they also need accommodation. But they cannot be raised in a family environment that is totally accommodating to their individual character: this makes good, sound sense because the world does not, of course, operate this way. The world makes demands for regularity, cooperation, and predictable behavior of everyone, and a family must prepare a child to live in the world.

It must be noticed that the concept of goodness of fit is a variation on the theme of moderation. Goodness of fit is another way of saying that extreme strategies, like forcing children to comply or caving in to their particular ways, are to be avoided at all costs, while good parenting is the business of negotiating between extremes. It is all the more complicated when one tries to apply the principle of goodness of fit to a large family; the idea that some children need more or less of something than others is hard to put into practice in a family of several children, because children always equate fairness with sameness. But nobody ever said good parenting was easy. It is about as easy as democracy: finding the delicate balance between liberty and order, or between compassion and efficiency, is a murky enterprise indeed.

THE CLARITY PARADOX

What we know about all this, then, is not new, and it is not always clear either. And the paradox of modern parenting is that as worrying increases, the wish for clarity also increases. Parents turn to scientific solutions out of a wish for clarity, and the more worried people are, the more they wish for a simple, clear answer. Indeed, anxious people are some of the most impulsive and concrete people there are; people who are truly overwhelmed with anxiety, in a clinical sense, often make bad judgments or fall for simple solutions because simple solutions promise an end to overwhelming anxiety. The clarity paradox is this: as parenting becomes more worrisome, people seek more clarity and simplicity, but clarity and simplicity are probably not entirely helpful. They are always the product of extreme theories. The right answers are probably not things like "Never, never take your child into your bed with you" or "Never, never spank your child." The right answers are more likely things like

"Never take your child into bed with you except when she or you really need it" or "Never spank your child unless he really won't get the message any other way." These kinds of answers lack the clarity that worried people seek.

But psychology does have something else to offer. It has great traditions of clinical theory and expertise to help with the problem of worrying. While we are feeling our way along in this confusing world, we can use what psychology offers as signposts that we have too long ignored; we can use strategies for evaluating risk, and our knowledge of our own values and wishes, as guides to help us find our way through the murk.

Three

THE MANAGEMENT
OF WORRYING:
THERAPEUTIC TRADITIONS

In 1932, theologian Reinhold Niebuhr penned the famous Serenity Prayer, which was subsequently adopted by Alcoholics Anonymous meetings all over the world. The familiar prayer is a poignant call for help, but it also contains a simple rule for the management of worrying: "God, grant me the serenity to accept the things I cannot change, courage to change the things I can, and wisdom to know the difference." The genius of the Serenity Prayer is that it captures the simplicity of managing life's difficulties, but it also captures the fundamental impossibility of managing those same difficulties—because, of course, knowing the difference between what we can and cannot change is the ability that most of us, especially chronic worriers, lack. While the Serenity Prayer is something of a paradox, it still has provided comfort and guidance for millions and has proven to be of real and practical significance.

When it comes to contemporary parenting, however, the Serenity Prayer has been largely discarded. Although the prayer does not prescribe total passivity, it does prescribe passivity when passivity is warranted. And passivity is a value, or a stance with respect to the difficulties of the world, that has disappeared from the lexicon of contemporary parents. "I'd do anything for my kid," parents say to me regularly. "When it comes to my kids, I'll fight to the death," another parent says. "My kids mean everything to me." "My kids come first." Self-sacrifice for one's children is a universal parenting value, but in contemporary America the proclamation of this value has been elevated to a personal creed; it is a way of knowing who we are, and a way of proclaiming our membership in the Good Parents Club. Members of the Good Parents Club have their own version of the Serenity Prayer, which goes something like this: "God, grant me the courage to change the things I can change for my child, and the courage to change what seems to be unchangeable for (or about) my child, and the courage never to see any difference."

In the parents I meet, these two values, wise passivity and parental self-sacrifice, are in conflict, but wise passivity is definitely losing. One can speculate about the reasons for this, and the fact that the Serenity Prayer is a prayer points in one direction. If a parent is in a relationship with a divine presence of whatever sort, and that divine presence is even remotely protective, the parent can share the burden of child protection with the deity. Here, too, we can turn to the example of how and why Alcoholics Anonymous works for so many people. When alcoholics "turn over" a burden of worrying or anxiety, they turn it over to their Higher Power; the fantasy of human omnipotence is described as a major feature of the disease of alcoholism, and the cure for that symptom is embracing wise passivity, by recognizing the omnipotence of a Higher Power. One could certainly argue that, in a secular culture, parents who are not in a relationship with a protective deity are much less likely to embrace wise passivity; if there is something threatening our children, many of us feel we need to go it alone to do whatever it takes to protect them. Those parents who can count on a divine presence to help out might be less likely to need to do it all themselves.

But increased secularism is only one reason why wise passivity is in decline. We can also speculate about this decline in an evolutionary sense. Scientists who study self-sacrifice in the world of nonhuman animals have long pointed out that parental self-sacrifice makes sense as an evolutionary strategy only in certain limited ways. In the most extreme cases, a parent may give up his or her (usually her) life to protect the young. But if the evolutionary Golden Rule is "Get as many of your genes into the gene pool as possible," sometimes parental self-sacrifice is not the best strategy. In organisms that have many offspring, or have the potential to have many offspring, it makes no evolutionary sense for parents to sacrifice themselves for any one of those offspring; parents need to preserve themselves to feed and care for all the rest of their actual or potential offspring. This is, in fact, the most efficient way of getting as many genes into the gene pool in subsequent generations.

So what about the evolutionary converse? If a parent has few offspring, and does not have the (conscious) plan to have any more offspring, what would we expect of that parent? In the wild, if an animal had only one offspring over the entire course of its reproductive life, we would imagine that that animal would be more likely to sacrifice herself if necessary to protect the offspring; the only way to keep those genes in the gene pool at all is to make sure that offspring survives at least until the age of sexual maturity. This animal's rule for living would, in fact, be very much like the Good Parents Club version of the Serenity Prayer. Evolutionary psychology tells us that, as parents have fewer and fewer offspring, protective activity on the part of parents will increase; an animal in the wild with only one offspring might just not be destined to be serene.

This may be a good evolutionary strategy, until such time as the eternal vigilance, the worrying, if you will, of that parent starts to interfere with the offspring's ability to develop normally. If the vigilance of the parent interferes with the offspring's ability to thrive, the strategy has lost its evolutionary value. This interference could come about if the vigilance so exhausts the parent that he or she loses the ability to protect the offspring. It could also fail if the parent loses the ability to discriminate between real and imagined dangers, or if the offspring is so protected that it does not develop the ability to function without the protection of the parent. In either case, the offspring's ability to survive and get its genes into the gene pool is compromised, and so the strategy of eternal vigilance has outlived its usefulness.

❖   ❖   ❖

And once again, we come to the limits of evolutionary psychology. It is provocative and rich with imaginary possibilities to see ourselves, as Desmond Morris did, as "naked apes." It also might go some way to suggest why contemporary parents have so much difficulty turning over any parental function, or embracing wise passivity.

There are things about our children, and about the world they live in, that we can change and some things we cannot change, and we would certainly be more serene if we knew those differences. But there are also things about *ourselves,* as parents, that we can change. We can change the way we think about the dangers our children are exposed to, and we can become less worried in the process. But in order to do that, we need to abandon evolutionary psychology as a guide for living—after all, it has only one prescription for parental worrying, and that is to have more children. If we are not ready to embrace that prescription, we can turn to the world of human psychology, which provides two rich therapeutic traditions for the treatment of worrying, psychoanalytic therapies and cognitive-behavioral therapies. It turns out that both those traditions can point us in a useful direction.

PSYCHOANALYSIS
AND ANXIETY

As in any good therapeutic school of thought, the psychoanalytic prescription for curing anxiety is linked to a theory of how people get so anxious in the first place. This tradition is long and multifaceted, and cannot be reviewed in its entirety here. But the principles of anxiety management are relatively simple; indeed, some would argue that the explanatory theory of psychoanalysis has so permeated American culture that we no longer recognize it as such: what was once radical Freudian psychology is now seen as common sense.

Psychoanalytic discussions of anxiety rest upon a distinction that is simple enough to make, although difficult to realize in practice. Anxiety is experienced when a person's sense of real danger is exaggerated or displaced. The term "fear" is used to mean the emotion appropriate to the real danger, and "anxiety" is what's added on—the emotion that is irrational because it is disproportionate to the real danger.

This definition conforms to the pattern of all early psychoanalytic definitions: it assumes that there is a rational, efficient mode of functioning in the world and there is no need to investigate or explain any further when all that is working well. When you *can* remember someone's name correctly, there is no need to invoke a psychoanalytic explanation; it's when you can't that people start talking about Freudian slips. The boilerplate psychoanalytic explanation—an upwelling of an unconscious wish or impulse—is used only to explain cases of the failure of ordinary, rational process. For example, if a woman calls her current husband by her ex-husband's name one too many times, that's when everybody starts to wonder why.

Anxiety, in this view, operates according to the same principles. A normal assessment of threat is just that: normal, rational, and appropriate to the degree of danger, whatever that might be. When there is an excess of worrying about the degree of threat, or worrying about something that is not a threat at all, psychoanalytic theory has always raised the possibility that there is something else going on: another thought, wish, impulse, or fantasy that is unpleasant to think about and is therefore repressed. It is this repression that adds the irrational element to the conscious experience of threat or danger.

This kind of explanation for worrying is pretty standard in parenting contexts. Take, for example, the mother who is terrified about her daughter's behavior on a date with a new, attractive boyfriend. She might worry excessively about whether her daughter will lose her head and go too far sexually. There is a real danger here—the daughter might in fact go too far, although let's assume for the sake of argument that she hasn't gone too far yet, so there is also good reason to assume she won't. But the extra anxiety—the part that is exaggerated or irrational—might come from some other feeling in the mother that, because it is embarrassing, is partially conscious or truly unconscious.

If I were the mother's therapist, I might be asking a question like "Why do you think she'll suddenly lose her head?" If the mother responded, "I know how girls act with a handsome guy like that," I might say, "How do you know?" One simple answer to my second question, probably readily available to consciousness, is "I know how I acted when I was her age." Other answers, possibly less available to consciousness, might be things like "I know how I acted when I was her age . . . and I still feel guilty about it" or "I know how I would act if I were going out with that cute guy" or even "I know what I would like to do with that cute guy." The further we go with this, the more we leave the real daughter, and the real danger to the real daughter, behind.

Parents always use simple projection when they try to figure out their kids' behavior. It is as natural as breathing to use "What would I have done at that age?" as a way of trying to understand what a kid might be up to. But the problem with this way of thinking is that it shades over imperceptibly (and eventually unconsciously) into thinking about *what I did when I was a kid and how I feel about it.* And so it is easy for parents to wander inadvertently into the territory of whatever bad feelings they might have left over from their own childhood or adolescence—often feelings of guilt, or anger, or sadness, or unacceptable longings.

We might actually be able to catalogue all the unspeakable feelings that might be expressed in the form of parental worrying. There are, of course, tons of things that we might wish for or long for that are truly unacceptable, and if the psychoanalytic theory of displacement carries any weight at all, we might usefully examine whether any of those other wishes are lurking under excessive parental concern.

To give another example, consider the big worry that plagues the families of high school students, that is, how to get the child into the prestigious college of our choice. This one is a big one, and in my experience, one that drives families crazy for several years running. I have sat with many families in which the son's failure to embrace a team sport in eighth or ninth grade is explicitly tied to failure in life because *(a)* failure to participate now means he won't acquire athletic skills, and *(b)* he won't make the junior varsity team in tenth grade, and therefore *(c)* he won't make varsity in his junior or senior year, and therefore *(d)* he won't get into the college of his choice, because even if he has good grades, good grades alone are not enough, and he doesn't seem to have any other talents or interests, and therefore *(e)* his wish to spend his time skateboarding now instead of practicing his layups is going to ruin his life. The worrying about the son's future seems straightforward enough, but it is certainly not difficult to come up with a covert wish or impulse that the parent might not be comfortable saying aloud but that might be driving the whole worry machine.

Like parents' own competitiveness. For some reason, even though it is seen to be good to be competitive at work, to be hard-driving and success-oriented, it is not okay to say aloud, "I want my son to go to an Ivy League school because I want him to triumph over the sons of my competitors. I want my business associates, and the guys at the golf club, and my brothers and sisters, to get that sick loser look on their face when they tell me their kid is going to the state university and I tell them my kid is going to Yale." Saying this aloud might be okay in places where clans are big and the success of one member of the clan is known to be shared by the entire clan, but Americans don't usually say this sort of thing aloud, at least not in public. That doesn't mean it hasn't been thought or felt, but it is not said. What is said is expressions of concern about the child's future, as if he has no future at all if he doesn't go to Yale. In fact, he probably has a fine future even if he doesn't go to Yale; what doesn't have a future is the parent's unseemly wish to grind his competitors into dust with his child's accomplishments.

REVIVING POLONIUS

In the chapters that follow, we will consider some of these worry amplifiers—parents' less-than-acceptable thoughts or feelings that ratchet up the worry in everyday life. There are many of these, and they are the sorts of things that therapists hear in moments when parents are being honest with themselves. In fact, they are heard very, very often if one practices in a therapeutic context that allows for these kinds of feelings to emerge.

But what is to be done about it? Short of undertaking one's own psychoanalysis as parenthood looms, what does psychoanalytic theory offer as a treatment for this kind of worrying? One thing that can be done is to listen to the advice given by a kindly, if flawed, literary dad, Polonius in Shakespeare's *Hamlet*. In the first act, Polonius is giving advice to his own son, Laertes. He says, "This above all: to thine own self be true, / And it must follow, as the night the day, / Thou canst not then be false to any man." The quotation has become a bromide, but if one stops to consider what advice is being offered here, it turns out to be advice that is truly worth taking. Polonius's advice suggests that honesty, and straight dealing with others, is necessarily predicated upon straight dealing with the self. As a piece of parenting advice, it may, once again, seem counterintuitive: After all, aren't we supposed to be thinking about *them,* our children, rather than ourselves? Isn't being self-absorbed as a parent really a bad thing?

Yes and no. Self-reflection does not have to be self-absorption. There are many routes to self-knowledge, including personal therapy, meditation, prayer, and any other type of conversational inquiry in which the self is the object of reflection. Knowing who you are, as a parent, and knowing what you really want, no matter how unspeakable, will open the way for much more clarity about all that worrying about your kids. The psychoanalytic theory of displacement simply suggests that the best treatment for worrying is knowing what the worrying is displaced *from* . . . and that is, very frequently, some wish or anxiety of our own. In the forthcoming chapters, we will consider some of those displaced anxieties as sources of excess worrying. In keeping with psychoanalytic theory, we'll call them the *fantasies* that drive parental worrying: not fantasies in the sense of longed-for things, but fantasies in the sense of not quite rational, sometimes unspeakable or unacceptable, sometimes pushed-out-of-awareness things that drive the worry machine. Don't worry: we'll also get to the facts.

THINKING ABOUT THINKING:
COGNITIVE-BEHAVIORAL THERAPY

The other great therapeutic tradition that has something important to say about parental worrying is cognitive-behavioral therapy, a form of psychotherapy that began in the 1960s and continues to grow in popularity and sophistication forty years later. The reasons for this continued growth are complex, but many have argued that this form of therapy is much more in tune with the American psyche than psychoanalytic therapy. It is not so concerned with dark, unspeakable motives, and not so concerned with history. It is concerned, instead, with results, with practical, achievable goals that can be realized in a fixed amount of time and with a fair expectation of success.

Cognitive-behavioral therapies were born, in a theoretical sense, in one book, indeed, in one chapter of one book. In 1967, the psychiatrist Aaron Beck wrote an enormously influential book on depression; in it, he reported the results of his research on the characteristics of depressed people. One chapter, "Cognitive Distortions in Depression," described the ways that depressed people think. Beck described the several logical errors made by persons suffering from depression, and described these thinking errors in a detailed fashion. One such thinking error is overgeneralization: a depressed person will typically draw a too-general rule from a single experience. Beck's clinical example of overgeneralization is this poignant description of one man's morning:

> A patient reported the following sequence of events occurring within a period of half an hour: His wife was upset because the children were slow in getting dressed. He thought, "I'm a poor father because the children are not better disciplined." He then noticed a leaky faucet, and thought that this also showed he was a poor husband. While driving to work, he thought, "I must be a poor driver or other cars would not be passing me." As he arrived at work, he noticed some other personnel had already arrived. He thought, "I can't be very dedicated or I would have come earlier." When he noticed folders and papers piled up on his desk, he concluded, "I'm a poor organizer because I have so much work to do."

Beck went on to argue that depression might not be the cause of such errors in thinking, but the result of such errors. The treatment for depression, then, should not be focused on the root causes of depressive feelings themselves, but should focus on changing the cognitive errors that lead to feelings of depression. In the example above, the focus of therapy might be on the act of overgeneralization itself, rather than the depressive conclusions that followed from these overgeneralizations. In the years since this book first appeared, cognitive-behavioral therapies have been used with success in the treatment of depression and especially anxiety disorders, and have also been adapted as a treatment for almost every other type of emotional disturbance and mental illness.

The relevance of cognitive-behavioral therapy for treating parental worrying is immediately apparent in the area of risk assessment. Indeed, one of the major habitual errors in excessive worrying is what these therapists call "probability overestimation," or mentally inflating the likelihood of a negative event. Pathological worriers, in this view, worry about many of the same things as everybody else, but they grossly overestimate the probability of occurrence of these things. In a similar fashion to overgeneralizers, pathological worriers assume that any single bad happenstance, anywhere, will probably happen to them next.

Another characteristic of pathological worriers, according to cognitive therapists, is that they frequently believe that worrying is an active treatment: they often feel that worrying itself is an activity that will forestall the dreaded event. The reason why many worriers have difficulty responding to treatment is that they are afraid to give up worrying, because worrying is seen as something good. There is, of course, a great deal of irrational thinking involved in this. Worrying about a potential plane crash ahead of time might have some marginal value if those worries motivate a person to study the relative safety records of several different air carriers, but once the plane is in the air, no amount of worrying is going to hold it up. Helping pathological worriers understand, and then give up, this thinking error is one of the central activities of cognitive-behavioral therapies for anxiety.

Risk assessment, then, is a central notion to both the

pathology and the treatment of worrying. Pathological worrying (most often described as "generalized anxiety disorder" in the *Diagnostic and Statistical Manual of Mental Disorders*, the bible of the American mental health profession) is identified by a failure of risk assessment. And one of the cognitive-behavioral treatments for the disorder is to help restore clients to normal worrying by retraining them in the skills of probability estimation.

If there has been, in the last decade or two, an upsurge in normal parental worrying, or parental worrying that is verging over into the pathological (and, like Freudians, cognitive-behavioral therapists struggle mightily to find ways to identify the dividing line between normal and pathological while acknowledging that this is like trying to draw a line on the surface of a pond), we might think about the trends in contemporary society that contribute to faulty risk assessment. One such trend is, of course, exposure to print and electronic media that contribute, in their very essence, to probability overestimation.

A good recent example was the trial of the "rink rage" father in the winter of 2002. The defendant, a Boston-area dad, was charged and eventually convicted of involuntary manslaughter for killing another father in an argument over a hockey game in which their sons were playing. The television coverage of this event was enormous; cable news outlets had extensive coverage, and every newspaper in the country had a front-page picture of the defendant on the witness stand, demonstrating just how he had delivered the fatal blows. The news coverage implied that this case had great relevance because of the more general issues involved, in this case, parents' overinvolvement in youth sports. But the coverage of the case was completely out of proportion to the prevalence of the phenomenon. Parents beating each other to death is not really a common phenomenon; it is, in fact, astonishing because it is so unique.

In the terms of cognitive-behavioral therapy, this coverage

is an excellent example of a pathological process: the enormous and widespread coverage of this event had the effect of focusing our attention, as a nation, on a problem in which the catastrophic outcome is extremely improbable. We are invited, by this type of coverage, to become pathological worriers, or are at least invited to participate in one of the most common thinking errors committed by pathological worriers. Many children play organized sports; some parents argue with each other or with coaches; almost no one beats anyone to death over these issues. And yet, exploiting the "chain of worry" described by cognitive-behavioral therapists is precisely what is done by this type of coverage. Marlene Dann, Court TV's senior vice president of daytime programming, was quoted in the *Boston Globe* after the trial as saying, "I think that people really identify with the issue. . . . Lots and lots of parents have been to many games, and we've seen it get out of hand. This is the worst-case scenario." But as cognitive-behavioral therapists keep trying to tell us, it is precisely the premature, irrational movement from little worries to worst-case scenarios that characterizes pathological worrying.

In the summer of 2002, the nation was treated to another such phenomenon, the "rash" of child abductions that horrified parents around the country. Graphic media coverage of the abduction and murder of Samantha Runnion in July, and the abduction and rape of two teenage girls in California in August, led to another outpouring of national anxiety about how to protect our children from this apparently increasing phenomenon. In fact, the quieter voices in the media were saying, at the same time the coverage was going on, that there is not and has not been an increase in the actual rate of child abductions. CNN news anchor Connie Chung even devoted an entire hour of her nightly news show to the statistical phenomenon, interviewing experts about the nonepidemic, even as her own network fed the national mood with round-the-clock accounts of individual abductions. Informed media consumers might notice that these pseudoepidemics always seem to take place in the summertime, when Congress is not in session and the president is on vacation. The abductions are tragic events, but they are extremely infrequent; they seem more frequent only when there is nothing else to talk about.

Healthy risk assessment, then, might be seen as a casualty of modern life. Just as increases in asthma or emphysema might be seen as a logical consequence of a constant exposure to smog, so we might conceive of pathological worrying as an exacerbation of a normal condition brought about by exposure to modern life. Those who are vulnerable to probability overestimation anyway will be pushed over the line by constant, detailed depictions of the most extreme news events; normal worrying becomes pathological worrying for more and more people, just as manageable allergies become pathological for more and more people when they are breathing too much polluted air.

The tendency for risks, real risks, to be distorted in the media is a big topic, and one that cannot be taken up completely here. A useful account of this phenomenon is that of sociologist Barry Glassner, whose 1999 book, *The Culture of Fear*, addresses the hyperbolic reporting of risks and dangers in American culture, including the risks posed by aggressive children, welfare mothers, predatory minority men, illnesses, plane wrecks, and just about every other modern "threat." For Glassner, the marketing of fear is a conscious project driven by the same thing that drives the marketplace: a profit motive. Advocacy groups are one culprit in the marketing of fear, according to Glassner, because making a minor social problem into a major social problem is one way of securing funding, whether from private or public sources. Glassner also points to aggressive fear mongering as a diversionary tactic in cases when addressing real threats might prove costly to some sector of the American economy. If, for example, the problem with kids shooting kids is an epidemic of violence-prone children, then we don't have to think seriously about limiting kids' access to what they are shooting one another *with*. In the aftermath of school shootings across the country in the late nineties, Glassner discusses overt attempts by gun manufacturers to spin this problem as a problem of child violence, and therefore not a problem of gun proliferation.

Academicians who specialize in the area of risk assessment are a great source of information about the difference between real and exaggerated threats to our children. There are real threats to children as a group, but those threats are not new or sexy; the threats to our children, as a group, are poverty and ill health, and the sequelae of these real dangers. Many threats to children are very easily addressed, and not hard to discover. For example, the Center for Risk Analysis at the Harvard School of Public Health is a source of information about real risks to children, and it also informs about useful things parents can do. These things are truly important, but not very edgy— things like seat belts and bike helmets and vaccinations.

The edgy threats are often the irrational ones, which really appeal to people's unspoken prejudices, while the associated real threats are just plain old money and politics. Another of Glassner's examples is the threat of "fatherlessness," the dangers for children inherent in growing up in a home without a father. The spooky, provocative version of this threat is cast in terms of the need for the firmness, guidance, and so forth, that only fathers can provide; we all have an atavistic conviction that children need a warm, supportive mother and a strong, demanding father in order to do well in life. Some research findings do appear to support the notion that children growing up in homes without a father do less well than other children. But the real situation of children growing up in a home without a father is that they have less money than children growing up in a home where a father is present; divorce settlements and many fathers' unwillingness to make adequate child support are a great contributor to child poverty in homes where there are no fathers. It is not easy to grow up in a home without a father, but the reason why it isn't easy can be genuine or it can be spurious, and the spurious concerns can have the effect of diverting attention from boring old social problems that refuse to go away. Glassner's argument reminds us that being aware of the reality of risks to our own children often means looking through hyperbolic rhetoric that aims to effect or prevent social change.

VIGILANCE, POWER, AND WORRYING

We can end this discussion of worrying where it began, by thinking again about the virtue of wise passivity. Cognitive-behavioral therapists tell us that it is hard for chronic worriers to stop because many of them see worrying as an active thing, a thing one does to actually protect the object of worrying. This is, in an objective sense, irrational. But parenting itself is a unique training ground for worrying because it teaches people to worry: it begins with a real, and useful, and not irrational activity, the activity of vigilance.

"Vigilance" is the word that best describes the activity performed by parents of infants. Parents of infants are always listening—listening for sounds that might mean trouble or danger. They are watching, always: they watch infants and toddlers all the time, to see if they are getting too near the electrical outlets, or the hot stove, or the stairs. This is why it is difficult to talk to a parent of an infant: they are only partly listening, while the other part of their attention is listening for sounds of disturbance, danger, warning, even when a child is asleep. Indeed, doctors who treat sleep disturbances know that very frequently parents, especially mothers, acquire sleep disturbances for the first time when they first have an infant, because they never really allow themselves to fall into a deep sleep.

Vigilance is not irrational; it is an active treatment, a good thing that parents do to keep infants and toddlers healthy. Mothers who do rescue children about to fall down the stairs, or children whose breathing changes when they have something stuck in their throat, are rewarded by experience: they are taught that vigilance is an active treatment. But vigilance, once learned in a situation with life-or-death consequences, is hard to turn off. It is *always* hard to turn off, and not just for parents. Just ask any war veteran who has spent time on sniper patrol or any other form of duty where vigilance is the thing that kept his comrades alive; these soldiers don't always put away the habit of vigilance when it is no longer necessary to be vigilant.

The first outing, or parental date, after a child's birth is a mythical turning point, or an episode for caricature, depending upon one's point of view, for precisely this reason. At the point when one leaves the house, and leaves the baby in the care of the baby-sitter, vigilance becomes irrational; no amount of thinking about what the infant is doing can help at that point. But that doesn't help most people in this situation, because the vigilance, which until ten seconds ago was totally useful and rational and has just become irrational, is not so easily turned off. One can even construct a coherent evolutionary argument for this phenomenon; in the days of our primate ancestors, parents, especially mothers, were probably pretty much on duty all the time; predators were always around, after all. So the ability to turn vigilance on and off may be an ability that humans are not really well adapted to, when it comes to children.

There is an old proverb, attributed to Eastern European Jewish culture, that says, "God couldn't be everywhere at once—that's why he made mothers." The reason this is funny, and true, is that the real truth of it is precisely the other way around, especially now. Mothers can't be everywhere at once— that's why they need God (or invent God—I cannot claim any authority on theological matters). Worrying is, for many people, the secular form of praying; instead of doing your part for your child, when you are apart, by asking God to protect him or her, you do the protection yourself, by worrying. It is irrational, but so close to the border of rationality that it hardly matters. Turning your child over to the care of others, being apart—these are the really difficult transitions for most parents. Eventually, you will turn the child over to him- or herself, and hope for the best. Until then, you try your best to turn off the worrying.

*　　*　　*

So, we can rely on psychoanalytic theory to uncover, or at least suggest, the fantasies that add to parental worrying. We can also rely on cognitive-behavioral theory to suggest methods for accurate risk assessment. Our topics, from here on, are some of the hot topics in contemporary parental worrying: substitute care, the effects of media culture, and overscheduling, to name just a few. I hope to take these hot topics and, with the aid of psychological theory, cool them off, so we can all find a little more serenity.

Four

OH, THOSE NASTY
DATE BOOKS

It is possible for normal, not-psychotic people to feel perse-
cuted by objects: the toaster that always burns the toast, the
dishwasher that breaks down on Thanksgiving. We all know
them and hate them. But there is one object that contemporary parents hate more than any other, and that is their date
book, or calendar, or personal planner, or, for those more technologically inclined, their Palm Pilot. Actually, we love them
and hate them at the same time; we certainly can't function
without them, and we're terrified if they're gone, but we hate
how much we need them. They're like the cell phone that gets
thrown overboard or the beeper that gets used to prop up a
table leg in a recent popular beer commercial: wouldn't it be
nice to just throw them away?

And what about our children's date books? Children's date
books are a relatively new phenomenon, but they do exist, even
if they are almost always carried by Mom in her oversized
carryall. Children's date books have become the symbol of the

overscheduled child, the bane of every worried parent's existence. In my clinical practice, I bump up against them most often when I am meeting a new patient who needs a weekly appointment. As a busy therapist, I don't have regular hours opening up every day of the week, and so there is a painful negotiation process that goes something like this:

> Me: I could see him Tuesday at four-thirty.
> Parent: Tuesday he has soccer until five, then he goes right to Cub Scouts.
> Me: Well, let's see. I will have an hour next week that might be regular, next Friday at four.
> Parent: Friday at four; let's see. That's his free day; he goes right from school to his guitar lesson, and then he's home by five. It's really his only free day. And when skiing starts, he'll be skiing every Friday.

And off we go. Now, as an aside, this is a terrible start to a child's psychotherapy. Most children enter therapy because they are having difficulty in school or in peer relationships, and no therapist in his right mind really wants to interfere with possibilities for after-school socialization or after-school activities that might make a child feel more successful than school makes him feel. It is much better to start a child's therapy without immediately creating a feeling of anger or deprivation in the parent by being rigid about schedules; parents are ambivalent enough about therapists as it is, and it doesn't help to start off with, "Well, the doctor says Johnny needs therapy, but the only time he can see him is right in the middle of play practice. I hate to have him give up something so important to him." Truth? Therapy will never be as fun as play practice.

But even when children don't need to see a therapist, therapists frequently hear parents' worries about their children's schedules. In fact, if there is one complaint a child therapist hears more than any other, it is this: our children have too much to do. "I wish they had more downtime." "There's never enough time to just hang out, or mess around." "I worry that they seem busier than we are." But if you listen closely, you will hear that this is always a two-part complaint. The first part is worrying about children's schedules, and the other part is nostalgia: "When we were kids, we had so much more time to mess around." "I remember just fooling around with other kids in the neighborhood when I was his age." The fully articulated complaint always boils down to the same formula: "When we were children, we could be free—but my child can't be free."

Stop long enough to notice here that children do not complain about this nearly as much as adults. There is an occasional child, usually a child who is depressed or terribly anxious, who really never wants to leave the house. But most kids, in my experience, like the things they do after school. They love play dates; they love soccer; they usually like music lessons or being in a play; they love Cub Scouts or Girl Scouts. The only thing they usually don't like is religious school, but most kids I know accept that one with a fair amount of equanimity because it is important to Mom and Dad. It is not primarily children who experience this worrying about scheduling, or long for those good old days with the neighborhood pack of friends. This worry, and especially this longing, is really a parents' thing. "When we were children, we could be free—but my child can't be free." Let's break this one down a little further: why, exactly, can't they be free, and why, exactly, do we feel we were so free?

"WHEN WE WERE CHILDREN, WE COULD BE FREE . . ."

Now for a little walk down memory lane. What is this nostalgia all about? It is so ubiquitous, in my experience, that it cries out for an explanation. (Have a counterexample? I am always available to stand corrected. Let me know if you have *ever* heard a contemporary parent say, "When I was a kid, we always had so many activities going on, I always felt hurried, so I always like to see my kid lolling around on the family room floor.") The report is always about a remembered golden age when, in the company of siblings or neighborhood friends, we made our own fun. I have such memories. As a child growing up in a suburbanish neighborhood in the making, I scampered about with my siblings and friends after school, building forts out of newly cut hay or fruit crates scrounged from the local grocery store. We fished for crayfish and turtles in the creek near our house, and tested one another to see who could run the fastest or climb the highest in tall trees. We also broke into every new house being built in the neighborhood and left little tokens of our presence. We spied on scary old neighbors, and committed major acts of trespass and minor acts of vandalism. When in our own houses with parents somewhere nearby, we occasionally wrote and performed our own plays; when outside, we occasionally shot other children with BB guns.

My point? Those lovely memories of unstructured time (and I think my own are representative of many of the memories I hear as a grown-up therapist) are actually pretty complicated and heterogeneous. There is certainly a lack of supervision in these memories. There are memories of some real accomplishments that seem very valuable because they were accomplished without adults, like the play we wrote and performed. There are also memories of some real mischief that could have been disastrous, and memories of a huge amount of time lolling about on the family room floor, watching television.

What is wonderful about these memories, and very different from the experience of contemporary children, is two major factors: the sheer size of play groups—there were always lots of children around, everywhere—and the blissful lack of adults bossing us around. I contend that these two factors are intimately related; whether or not times were actually safer (this is a question that may be answered by crime rates), parents felt safer letting children be out in the world, not because they didn't need supervision, but because *they were supervised by other children.* In my neighborhood, at least, there were children everywhere. A sneaky child molester might have succeeded, with persistence, but anyone who tried to snatch a child would have had to fight off a horde of siblings and neighbors. Children never walked to school alone, because there was no "alone." The parental standard may have been different in some less conscious ways; with more children in each family there might have been less frenetic investment in each and every child, and therefore parents may have been more casual about risks (see Chapter 1). But family size also affected child safety standards, because children were expected to look out for one another, and there was never a lack of children available to do so.

The hordes of unsupervised children I remember were not exactly innocent, if my own memories are at all representative. Nostalgic memories for the creative possibilities in unstructured time for children must, if they are honest, include the memories of creative ways to get into trouble. It is also true that the unsupervised games we feel our children have lost often looked a lot like supervised games. Playing baseball and football without an adult coach or referee was, and is, different from playing with an adult coach or referee, but not all that different; the cultural transmission was more indirect in that the rules were transmitted from father to older brother to younger brother to playmates, rather than directly from Coach. But the rules and the activity were largely similar, although there were the important differences of self-transportation and completely voluntary, and frequently sporadic, participation.

The other emotional difference in these memories is crucial, however: these "when I was a kid" memories of unstructured time are always about cooperation. The "we" in these memories is always a happy, rough-and-ready, but fair group of kids working together without help or interference from adults. The "we" in nostalgic memories is never the *Lord of the Flies* crowd, torturing the weak or different. It is as if all the aggression in our childhoods evaporated over the years. We messed around without adult supervision or planning, and nobody ever felt bad or got hurt. What we remember is the "we" of creative cooperation, not the "us versus them" of unfettered child aggression or competition.

And this, I would argue, is the heart of the matter regarding this nostalgic fantasy: as grown-ups who live in what feels like an increasingly competitive world, we are extremely ambivalent about competition. Americans work longer hours than anyone in the world, and as some authors have pointed out, it is the *adults* who feel stressed out and don't have enough down time (Juliet Schor, for example, makes this point elegantly in her 1991 book, *The Overworked American*). Many of us hate our own lives, or at least our own date books. This is why, after all, people make those commercials where the pager gets thrown into the deep blue sea. We like the advantages brought on by being busy, including more money, social contacts, and recreation, but we hate the pace, and the background insecurity, of unfettered market capitalism. We have lots of competitors in everything we do, from the grocery line to the realty office, and we hate to compete at the same time that we love to win.

It is a time-honored strategy to project one's anxieties onto one's children, and it's not the end of the world, as long as you know what you are doing. But in this case, let's take a good long look at this: we complain about our children's overburdened schedules, and we long for the golden years of our youth. The golden years of our youth, when all we did was cooperate, in a free and unrestricted way, with other children, is a fantasy: it is a projection of a wish to be free of competition now, in the present. We were not free of competition in the past, and if we are honest, we might remember some of the more terrible examples of competition with siblings and age-mates in our own past. It wasn't all that innocent, either; unsupervised children tend to get into trouble, and unsupervised children in the good old days got into good-old-days trouble just as unsupervised kids now get into new-century troubles. But the nostalgic fantasy keeps alive the wish that someplace there is an Edenic land where everyone gets along all the time, and all work is play, and no one gets into trouble.*

MY CHILDREN CAN'T BE FREE

Why do they need to do all this stuff anyway? Presumably, if parents decide that their child is doing too much, they can cut back on after-school or weekend activities and have more family downtime. None of this stuff is actually compulsory. But it *feels* compulsory, for two related, but distinct, reasons: the requirements of *accomplishment* and the requirements of *supervision*.

❋   ❋   ❋

Accomplishment. Consider the following anecdote found in a recent issue of *Boston* magazine. The writer, Ann Brochin, is giving a parent's account of applying to private elementary schools in the Boston area.

> "My son was 3 when I was told that I should start to worry. 'You are already behind the eightball,' a colleague confided one day in the supermarket aisle.
> " 'You had better get him in as a preschooler.' So many families in greater Boston chase so few private school slots that parents pester educational consultants for advice about how to 'package' their toddlers to improve their chances for admission. . . .

* For many people, this fantasy reached its collective zenith in the experience of Woodstock: "We are stardust, we are golden, and we've got to get ourselves back to the Garden." We might usefully remember that Woodstock was followed by Altamont, where bikers serving as security guards beat concertgoers to death. Or we may remember the destructive orgy that ended the Woodstock reunion concert in the year 2000. We might then be a little more careful about our memories of an idealized innocent past.

"Next came the applications. 'What are your child's interests?' they all asked. Wishing I could answer 'calculus,' I wrote: 'watching Disney videos.' "

This account is almost identical in form and content to accounts I hear several times a week. I don't want to push my child; I want my child to relax and have fun, *but I don't really have any choice, because my child's future is at stake.* My child can't be free, because he needs accomplishments—to get into private schools or to get into college. "The world is so much more competitive today" is the way I hear it from parents. Translation: "If he doesn't play soccer now, or excel at figure skating or the oboe, he won't get into an elite secondary school or college. And, if he doesn't . . ." The parent's voice trails off as he contemplates a bleak future for his child, flipping burgers at best.

The possibilities for catastrophic thinking here are enormous, and some attention to the facts of children's possibilities for success are clearly in order, to help fight off those poisonous fantasies of our children's future occupational failure. But trying to figure out what to do often involves the contemplation of the ubiquitous present as well. Parents often tell me that, although they wish their children and their family could have more unstructured time, they feel their child needs to "do something" because every other child is "doing something." Parents whose kids come home after school and mess around outside, in the woods or fields, or in the backyard, feel extremely defensive about these choices because they are now unusual. The reference to social norms becomes an end in itself, or a reason parents give themselves for why they lead such busy lives. Anxiety about choices is greatly reduced when one can feel that one has made the right choice, and one way of knowing the right choice is to examine what everyone else is doing. In this way, thinking about the catastrophic future for the child without accomplishments is unnecessary. One can simply think about what everyone else appears to be doing, and do the same thing. Children, of course, especially younger adolescents, always feel a tremendous pressure to fit in, to conform, so they will always weigh in on the side of a family choice that goes along with what everyone else is doing.

It is clear that the felt needs for children to have accomplishments have been institutionalized in modern family life, so that the messing-around child is not the norm. But there is another strain in modern parenting advice that suggests the dark side of the messing-around child: in a dangerous world (one that, as we all believe, is more dangerous than ever) unsupervised children are more likely to get into trouble.

*   *   *

Supervision. Another big reason why our children's after-school activities feel compulsory is the need for supervision. "The world is not as safe as it used to be," and therefore kids cannot be left on their own, in the house or out. Kids can get into more trouble than they used to (so the feeling goes), and so they need to be supervised; they cannot just hang out without an adult. And since they're going to be hanging out with an adult anyway, why not have them do something in a group so that not all the adults have to be on duty?

It is clear to anyone paying attention that many child experts constantly point to the need for children to be adequately supervised. Many child experts and those who collect statistics on juvenile crime have long noted that all the undesirable things children and adolescents can do frequently reach their peak in after-school hours, that is, the time when children are least likely to be supervised. Children need full date books so they don't pencil in "juvenile crime" on their own.

A good example of recent recommendations in this regard is those coming out of the Office of National Drug Control Policy, the federal agency responsible for combating drug use in the United States. A popular ad campaign for kids and parents in recent years featured the concept of the *anti-drug,* that is, any activity that makes a kid feel good and that he or she might use instead of drugs. Dr. Wade Horn, a child psychologist quoted on the ONDCP homepage, exhorted parents to "participate in positive alternatives to drugs by supporting activities and hobbies that become their children's 'anti-drugs.' " One print ad in the current campaign depicts a basketball court with a sign for a basketball clinic, and the following banner: SCIENTIFIC STUDIES HAVE SHOWN THAT MARIJUANA USE CAN BE PREVENTED BY TAKING YOUR KIDS TO THIS CLINIC.

To be fair, the national drug propaganda does not simply suggest that adult supervision *alone* is the anti-drug. The campaign suggests that adult supervision, *and* the supportive quality of adult contact, *and* the self-esteem that comes from real achievements like basketball are all factors that militate against drug use. Whether this campaign is or will be effective is not clear. It is notoriously difficult to track drug use at all, much less to evaluate a specific factor in an advertising campaign that might account for a change in drug use. But it is clear what this campaign is not: it is not a nostalgic view of unsupervised or unstructured downtime for kids. In the view of the anti-drug campaign, and the research that supports it, unstructured downtime for kids is a recipe for experimentation with drugs.

What these experts tell us is that children should not be alone, and that they should have real accomplishments (even if, or especially if, they are not doing well in school) that will promote self-esteem and keep them away from drugs. In the face of this advice, equally well intentioned but less scary admonishments about overscheduling or hurrying our children seem pale by comparison. One might argue that the relatively abstract arguments about the deleterious effects of overstructuring on children's cognition, contained in books like David Elkind's *The Hurried Child,* don't stand a chance against this kind of competition. And since "the world is so much more dangerous today," the risks of leaving kids alone seem infinitely more serious than they used to be.

❈ ❈ ❈

Both the needs of accomplishment and the needs of supervision, then, push families toward full date books for children. It is important to note, however, that the matter of whether the parents feel they have a choice here is vitally important. And parental choice in this matter may seem to improve the quality of life while also contributing to parental worrying.

For families where there is a nonworking parent at home after school (even if that parent works during school hours, he or she might be home after school), filling a child's schedule is primarily about the needs of *accomplishment*. After all, if a parent, usually Mom, is home after school, she can provide supervision. She could be the mom quietly in the background watching out for the children so they don't get into trouble but also not intervening or structuring their activity. She could be, if she chose, the mom of the good old days, who let her children mess around as much as they wanted to.

For these families, scheduling children for activities outside the home becomes a matter of choice, and therefore a matter of worrying about the rightness of the choice. Families who do not have an available after-school parent have a completely different set of worries they bring to the picture. The needs of *supervision* are paramount for those families who have none, and families who have elementary or junior high school students who are coming home to an empty house are much less ambivalent about scheduling their kids after school. They want their kids supervised, and although these families sometimes grieve that their kids do not have enough time to relax at home, they are usually extremely grateful if their child has a program to go to every day after school, whether it is the Boys or Girls Club, the YMCA, or the local public school's after-school program.

In thinking about these issues, it is important, especially for those of us with nostalgic fantasies about unstructured child-hoods, to remember that kids who attend after-school programs are very often in a loosely structured atmosphere. Many after-school programs are like big family homes, and they offer a wide variety of choices for kids, from supervised ball games to hanging around playing board games or cards, or just talking with friends. The supervision in many of these programs, especially the good ones that can create a family atmosphere, is like old-fashioned, laid-back child supervision. It can be one soccer game after another, but it doesn't have to be. Supervision, in other words, is not the same as overscheduling.

The psychological reasons for, and the psychological qualities of, out-of-school activities can be quite different for families in different circumstances. For the purposes of argument, we can separate accomplishment, which suggests optional, structured, disciplined activities that parents freely choose for their children to ensure a good future (and because everyone else they know is doing it), and supervision, which suggests less-optional arrangements based upon the current need for child safety, with less focus on structure and discipline and possibly more emphasis on quietly supervised downtime. The problem is that, for most people, these distinctions are not so clear. For example, anti-drug propaganda that promotes after-school activities as an inoculation against drugs doesn't make these distinctions clear at all. In fact, these advertisements suggest that a real accomplishment, like being able to play basket-ball, *over and above the adult supervision on the basketball court,* will also help kids stay off drugs. So even if you have a choice, and don't need to send your kid to a supervised after-school program because you're home after school, you might be a little worried about not having them do *something* to de-velop an accomplishment.

Decisions about what to do with kids outside of school hours also need to take into account what it feels like for kids, and for the adults who are spending time with them. Kids need supervision so they don't get into trouble, but they can be supervised at home, or in small groups, with any responsible adult. Being home lolling about in the family room *in the presence of a supervising adult* meets the supervision requirement. Shopping for the family dinner, cooking, painting the house with Dad or Mom after school, doing homework in a parent's presence—all these meet the criteria for adequate supervision. Some parents like nothing better than to quietly be in the house, quietly watching their children invent their own lives.

But some parents don't like hanging around the house and supervising, although it's kind of hard to say so. A big reason why the needs for accomplishment and supervision get confused is that many parents get bored and lonely hanging around with their children. So they supervise their children by hanging around the sidelines of a soccer game with other parents, and they feel less lonely. As far as I'm concerned, no human being needs to apologize for the need for human community; that's part of the humanity thing. If parents are saying, in effect, "I know my child needs supervision and I prefer to supervise him while I see my friends at the soccer field or the waiting room of the music school at the same time," that is perfectly okay. What is less okay with me, because it is less honest, is the following: "I get bored and lonely supervising my child at home so I'm going to get them and myself involved in a group activity . . . *but I'm going to pretend that it's all because of what they need.*" Then, instead of the parent feeling guilty because of a little enlightened self-interest, the child can feel guilty about how the parents are running themselves ragged on his behalf when he hears them complain about his schedule.

Almost every child I talk to likes after-school activities, structured or unstructured. One big reason they like them is that children do not like to be lonely. We should not forget, especially those of us who harbor feelings about our childhood Eden, that if we grew up in a larger family than the one our children are growing up in, we were probably less lonely hanging around the house. Indeed, there is a reason why so many only children say to me, "One thing I know for certain is that when I have kids I want to have more than one." Kids who are the only child in the house, or kids who have one sibling who is much older or much younger and is therefore not a good playmate, or, to a lesser degree, kids whose only sibling is of the opposite sex, frequently feel lonely after school. They don't really care if they are playing soccer, or playing in an orchestra, or playing Monopoly at the community center, but they do care about being able to have time *with playmates.* Some of our nostalgic feelings for our youth are, again, relatively simple projections of the lived experience of being a part of a larger generation, only this time it is the good part of that: there was always somebody around to play with. Parents in previous generations did not have to schedule play dates or drive hither and yon so that their children could have playmates. Smaller family sizes, in whole generations of people, mean smaller neighborhoods and fewer companions readily available. There is a reason, after all, that so many kids make a beeline for their computers to get on the instant messaging network as soon as they get home. They don't want to be lonely any more than we did when we were kids. The pressure that comes from them is not accomplishment, or supervision, but plain old companionship.

OVERSCHEDULED KIDS:
THE FANTASIES

The fantasies, remember, that we are discussing here are not necessarily much desired improbable outcomes, like winning the lottery or dating a celebrity. Fantasies, in this psychological sense, are all those irrational, unthought, or simply unspoken things that give the extra oomph to parental worrying. The issue of child overscheduling gives us plenty of fantasy material, which parents will sometimes articulate, especially in the safety of a therapeutic encounter. Here are two of the biggies:

"I want to win, and I want my child to win." These fan-

tasies are captured, for example, in the frequently heard statement that a child's acceptance to college and the quality of that college are one's "final exam" as a parent. As a therapist whose work always involves a dialogue with imagined others, some of whom are pretty punitive, my first question is, who's administering that exam? Who is evaluating you based upon the quality of the college that your child eventually attends?

The answer to that one is, of course, the parents' own parents, or the parents' own siblings. It is clear to most of us, in our more candid moments, that our final exam grade is one that we compare to others': those of our own siblings and our generational siblings, our friends and our children's friends' parents. And in fantasy, we want to bring our good grades home to Mom and Dad, just as we always did. As a therapist who also sees adults, I am frequently privileged to hear parents' feelings of triumph or unmanageable envy or shame after those final exam grades come in every spring. For some parents, it is an insufferable narcissistic injury to have gone to a state college or relatively unselective public university and to *not* have their child attend an elite private college. Just about every adult I know still knows his SAT scores, and still harbors resentments about any college that rejected him.*

"I hate how much I have to compete." The feeling that "the world is so much more competitive today" is often a statement about a parent's own life. Many parents' lives are extremely competitive, and globalization and worldwide economic competition are accelerating that trend. For many people, the world of security they remember is not a secure, unpressured childhood of their own, but a memory of the secure, unpres-

---

* One recent, and hilarious, example was a televised episode in which Comedy Central star Ben Stein, a former speechwriter for Richard Nixon and a man who constantly touts his own intellect, was interviewing fellow comedian Al Franken. In this interview, Stein went on at considerable length about why Franken was admitted to Harvard and Stein was not. This between two extremely successful men in their fifties.

sured job history of their own parents, in the era before we all had 4.2 career changes over the course of an average life.

If competitive feelings are in some direct proportion to the size of the group one is competing with, it would make sense that those of us raised in larger families or generations might feel much more competitive than those raised in smaller families or generations (see Chapter 1). Over the course of their lives, our children may not have to compete as much, and in every way, as we did. Economic competition may be accelerating, but the felt experience of competition may be quite different for our children. Except in those increasingly rare big families, our children will never have to compete the way we did, at least in the all-important competition for the resources of parental time and attention. They have plenty of that, and they always will.

Parents who are worrying about overscheduling need to think about their own relationship to nostalgic fantasy. They also need to think about competition in their own lives: Does it feel good? Does it feel overwhelming? Isn't there anything that parents can do to address these issues without projecting them onto children? What about throwing that beeper into the deep blue sea?

OVERSCHEDULED CHILDREN:
THE FACTS

As I discussed in Chapter 3, one good treatment for worrying is to examine the risks associated with terrible imagined outcomes of parental decisions. If worrying is characterized by inadequate risk estimation, or the overestimation of catastrophic outcomes, one good treatment is to examine some of the relevant data. Any casual student of social science will remember, of course, that statistics are to some degree always served up in the interest of persuasion. Oliver Wendell Holmes's famous dictum about "lies, damned lies, and statistics" is always relevant. The facts selected in this section, and in every similar section in the following chapters, were chosen with a persuasive purpose in mind: to help parents not to feel so terrified about their children's eventual fates.

With regard to overscheduling, we can examine the facts behind the separate rationales of accomplishment and supervision. Parents who don't want their children to feel overscheduled but feel that their children need accomplishments are almost always looking ahead to college admissions as the catastrophic end point of current sluggishness: no tennis team now, no Princeton later. But what are the facts about college admissions, and the outcomes of *that* particular ordeal?

Here's some data: the *U.S. News & World Report* college rankings, which are now received annually by anxious parents with roughly the same response as that garnered by the Ten Commandments. Looking at the 2001 ratings, we find a handy table of college rankings and acceptance rates; the *U.S. News* survey includes a measure of how hard it is to get in (as measured by the percentage of people accepted compared to all that apply). For the purposes of this brief look, we can turn to the "Top 50 National Universities" and the "Top 50 National Liberal Arts Colleges," arguably the top one hundred institutions of higher learning in the country (I say arguably because there is indeed a lot of argument about the validity of these rankings, but you'll have to take that up with other experts). In the national universities category, number-one Princeton and number-one Harvard (it was a tie in 2001) had acceptance rates of 11 percent, a fairly daunting prospect. But number-ten Cornell accepted 33 percent of applicants and number-ten (another tie) University of Chicago accepted 48 percent. There are sixteen universities in the top fifty with acceptance rates over 50 percent, including my dear old alma mater, the University of Wisconsin–Madison (number thirty-five in rankings, 74 percent acceptance rate). Tulane University and Yeshiva University, tied at forty-fifth in the rankings, also tied at 78 percent acceptance rates.

In liberal arts colleges, the story is a little more, well, liberal. Number-one Amherst accepted 19 percent of applicants, number-four Wellesley accepted 46 percent of applicants, and so on. There are twenty-three of the top fifty liberal arts colleges that accepted over 50 percent of applicants, including number-twelve Smith College, number-sixteen Bryn Mawr, and number-fourteen Grinnell. The fiftieth-ranked liberal arts college in the country (according to *U.S. News*), Willamette College in Oregon, had an acceptance rate in 2001 of 90 percent of applicants.

Parents can and will, of course, read the data through their own particular prism of worry. The way I read it, it's hard to get into the top five colleges in the country, but even in the top fifty there are colleges that aren't really rejecting people in droves. So, how many accomplishments does a kid need to get into college? These data suggest that the answer is, not as many as you think.

Okay, so it's sort of hard, or sort of not hard, to go to a good college. Is there data that would suggest that going to a good college is better, in terms of preparation for life, than going to a less-good college? This would require data that broke down postcollege income by tiers or ranks of colleges (controlling, meanwhile, for other factors that might contribute to postcollege income independently of the selectivity of the college itself). This kind of research is hard to come by, but there is some. A 1999 study by Caroline Hoxby of Harvard University and the National Bureau of Economic Research broke down colleges by ranks in the eight-category *Barron's* magazine rankings, and looked at lifetime income associated with attending selective colleges. When controlling for student aptitude, Hoxby found that the lifetime income advantage of attending a rank-one college over a rank-three college is approximately $100,000. The lifetime income advantage of attending a rank-two college over a rank-four college is $200,000. Hoxby makes the point that, rationally, a child with a choice should maximize his return by attending a more selective college, and indeed the data are robust seen in that light. In another light, if the *lifetime* economic advantage to be gained by going to Harvard or Princeton versus Colorado College or Macalester College (in *Barron's* rank three) is $100,000, is it worth driving yourself crazy about your child's accomplishments? Hoxby's analysis does not even include the cost of music lessons, or gas driving to soccer games, or gymnastics coaching, or SAT coaching, or whatever it is that makes a child desirable to a tip-top college, so her dollar figure probably overestimates the lifetime economic advantage. More important for our argument here is the emotional cost: if parents are constantly terribly worried about securing accomplishments for their children in order to get them into college, the real economic advantage of $100,000–$200,000 over a lifetime might at least place a value on all that worry. The facts, such as they are, are real enough, but how to act on them is another question.

Under the rationale of the need for supervision, the facts tell a different story. For example, in 1997, James Alan Fox, an expert on juvenile crime at Northeastern University, compiled FBI statistics that demonstrated that one half of all violent juvenile crime is committed between the hours of 2 and 8 P.M., and the rate of juvenile crime increases threefold between the hour from 1 to 2 P.M. and the hour from 3 to 4 P.M. on every school day. So there are those good reasons not to let the kids hang out, and to put something else in their date books beside violent crime. Other researchers in the field of child welfare have noted that one of the best predictors of juvenile delinquent status, including arrests and incarcerations for violent crime, is inconsistent or inadequate supervision of children. This supervision can be inadequate, of course, even if an adult is present; a parent who is at home asleep or mesmerized by Jerry Springer while the kids are upstairs smoking pot is not really an exemplar of good supervision, even if he is telling himself he is a good parent because he is home with his kids. The data speak loud and clear that kids need some kind of good adult supervision in order to stay out of trouble. It was ever thus, and it is still the case. But, as we have seen, supervision does not require overscheduling. It simply requires being there, being awake, and paying attention.

❊   ❊   ❊

The reality is that kids probably don't need as many accomplishments as we think they do; they'll get into some college, and probably a good one if they have good grades. And we might profit from an honest admission that we really like it when we triumph over our internal examiners or our external siblings when the kid gets into Hotchkiss or Choate or Harvard or Princeton, but over a long lifetime, it probably won't make that much difference to the kid (perhaps $5,000 extra per year over the course of a forty-year working life). They don't need accomplishments for big career advantages. They might want them for self-esteem, and they certainly need supervision in any case. Parents who have a choice, and who worry about overscheduling their children, can supervise them at home after school, and those who don't want to be home that much can supervise them with the other folks at a soccer game. Parents who need to work and need after-school supervision can find, if they are lucky, a program in which their children are supervised, which may or may not contain adult-structured activities. But no one, nohow, is going to bring back a world that never existed: the world where children always got along, without adults, and nobody got hurt or felt bad, and adults didn't have to compete but always won just the same.

If we feel terrible about this loss, we can still console ourselves in the knowledge that our children won't have to give up this fantasy either: when they are adults, they can remember, if they choose, the unstructured, undirected moments when they and their playmates were getting along, and imagine that their whole childhood was like that. If they feel traumatized by their busy lives (and I see no evidence that they will) they will distort the past the way we all do. They might forget all the efforts we made to give them their accomplishments and to keep them supervised, and remember instead how happy they were when they were just messing around. Who cares about the facts, as long as they're happy, right?

Try This at Home

1. Write a catalogue of all the terrible things you did when you were messing around without adult supervision in your Edenic youth.
2. Talk with your friends and siblings about the wonderful things you did without adult supervision when you were a kid. Write a memoir, if you wish. Memorialize a time in history that is never coming back. Celebrate the great things you did, and try to imagine that your children can go on living in a different world—a world in which they will not have all the great things you had, but a world in which they will have different great things.
3. Examine your own feelings about hanging out with your kids: do you like this activity? Do you get lonely or bored before they do? Do you ever say they need to do more stuff when it is really you that need to do more stuff?
4. If every adult in your home works after school, and your child is in a good after-school program, thank your God or your lucky stars. And if you have a choice in this regard, also thank your God or your lucky stars. The kids who really need worrying about are those who have no after-school supervision, even if their parents desperately want it.
5. Make a list of all the really successful people you know who went to public colleges. Make another list of all the people you know who went to superselective colleges and went nowhere in life.
6. Start a savings account, and put away $2,500 per year every year for your child. If you worry that they will not

get ahead in life because they might not go to a private college, you can give them this money instead, to make up for it.

7. Take a day off and loll around on the family room floor.
8. Most important, try to look at your child and try to listen for and observe what his after-school activities mean *to him.* If you really know this, you can act accordingly. You can ignore the worrying about what everyone else is doing because you will know what to do for him, for yourself, and for your family.

Five

TROUBLE IN
AU-PAIRADISE

Laura, a mother of twins who are in the fourth grade, has a decision to make. She has a chance to go back to her old job as a nurse, which she left when she had her children. She loved the work, and the family could use the money, but she is worried about how her return to work will affect her children. She will have flexible shifts and coverage for some after-school hours, but that is not her primary concern. Her primary concern is what it will mean to her children for her to give her attention to a job. "Even when they're at school, I'm always available," she says. "If I go back to work, I won't be. All I've ever wanted is to be there for my children."

Hearing this, it is impossible not to feel the sadness and the worry that go along with this statement. It is hard to know which is worse for parents: when a mother needs to go back to work and therefore has no choice about seeking substitute care, or when a mother wishes to go back to work and is trying to balance her own needs against what she perceives to be the needs of her children. As we have already seen, the burden of parental worry is sometimes worse when there are too many choices; and sometimes not having a choice, as painful as that is, frees a parent from the guilt that fuels this anxious transition. After all, if I *must* go back to work, I cannot be blamed for having made a selfish choice, right?

In either situation, choosing or not being able to choose to return to work, parents frequently feel stuck with one of the hardest decisions a parent can make in the lives of their children. But after noticing and feeling and recognizing this sad worrying, I start thinking about the statement "I just want to be there for my children." Be where? This is obviously more than a statement of location; it is not just wanting to be physically there. It is a wish to be psychically there, available, present, attuned, a wish to be *with* one's child. This wish is a pretty complicated package.

For many parents, a big part of this wish, and the worrying that goes along with it, is the wish not to miss anything. This is one of those worries that are real, and very important to parents, but it is one of those worries that parents have for themselves. For parents whose children are in substitute care from the time they are very young, the sadness about missing a child's first social smile or a child's first steps is a very big deal. Missing developmental milestones is an occasion for an enormous sense of loss for many parents, especially with a first child. (Children don't usually feel this sense of loss until later, and then it can become very important to them also.) Adults in therapy sometimes describe the sense of loss and anger that attends memories of children's achievements that they were not there to witness. (Helpful hint: if it ever occurs to you that it won't matter if you skip your child's school play, awards night, or high school graduation, think again.)

But this phenomenon, too, is affected by family size; families with more children tend to get less sentimental about these events. In larger families, one can note (with humor, if the family can take it) that first children's developmental milestones are always well documented. The baby book, with the diary of every day, and the pictures of each important event, and the sense of historic occasion that adheres to each new achievement, gets shorter and shorter with each successive child. You can always tell the birth order of a child, even without asking, while taking a developmental history: when a professional asks about first words, first steps, or toilet training, and the parents laugh and say, "I really don't remember," it's almost always a third or later child.

Beyond this sense of being there as a witness and celebrator of a child's life, what do parents mean when they say, "I just want to be there for my child"? If, after all, a child is in nursery school, or some kind of supervised program, even if for just a few hours a week, the parent is, usually by definition, "not there." The child is dropped off, and the parent goes away, and someone else is looking after the child. As we noticed in Chapter 3, many parents have the residual habit of vigilance and feel they are still on duty, even after the child has been dropped off or the baby-sitter has come in to the home. It is a parent's job to still "be there," in a psychological sense, thinking about the child, so that nothing bad happens to him or her. It's impossible to work anyway, right? You can't concentrate on your work, because it is your job to be there. It is this sense of absurdity that makes the process laughable or tragic, depending on the family. Parents say to themselves, and to each other, "Since I can't think about anything else anyway, why don't I just spend the time with my child and save him the trauma of being looked after by someone who is not his parent? After all, being a parent is a full-time job."

The magic of firsthand parenting is the subject here. One of the themes I hear over and over in parents' worries is the necessity for parenting to be done by the real, honest-to-God parent of a particular child. Just as parents say, "I want to be there for my child," and assume that everyone knows what that means, many parents also say, in a tone of firm disapproval, "I'm not going to let anyone else bring up my child." Case closed. We all know that's bad. Or something. We're all sup-posed to know what it means. But what does it mean? There is a certain magic in these words, something preemptive, like a force of nature. True, parenting *is* a force of nature, but it doesn't hurt every now and then to try to understand the words, even when powerful forces are invoked; it might even help, be-cause when parents invoke these preemptive forces, they feel terribly worried later when it's time to thwart them.

It will be useful here to take a little detour for a history les-son. Nothing is more salutary, as a treatment for parental wor-rying, than a stroll through the history of childhood in general and child care arrangements in particular, or a cross-cultural review of child-rearing practices. When one takes such a view, as, for example, in Philippe Ariès's 1962 classic, *Centuries of Childhood*, or, more recently, in the work of historians of child-hood like William Kessen, it is immediately apparent that par-enting has for most of human history *not* been a full-time job. Making a living has been the full-time job for most able-bodied adults because, in most of human history and in most parts of the world now, finding the resources to provide food and shel-ter for the parents themselves and the children requires that both parents work at something other than child care. Most often, this economic necessity means that if anybody is looking after children as a full-time job, it is people who cannot do full-time, physical, survival-related work. The people who do full-time child care, most of the time, are grandmothers or older siblings. Mothers themselves look after the children with a certain amount of divided attention while they do their own survival-related work. It is possible to take some amount of comfort from the fact, so clearly documented by historians or anthropologists of childhood, that the human race has bumped along fairly successfully with substitute care—that is, children being cared for by someone other than their own mother or father—as the rule and not the exception throughout most of human history.

Indeed, the entire enterprise of thinking about what children need has been described by some child development experts as a relatively new phenomenon, brought about by very specific changes in the economic order of the Western world. Jerome Kagan, a preeminent developmental psychologist at Harvard University for the last five decades, describes this process in his wonderful summation of thinking about children, *Three Seductive Ideas*. Kagan argues that contemporary thinking about child rearing as a uniquely important process happened when both mothers and children were freed from the necessity of the physical labor to ensure family survival.* Kagan writes:

In eighteenth-century Europe . . . a growing number of wives of merchants and skilled artisans were gradually freed of the responsibility of gathering wood, picking berries, tending domestic animals, and weeding vegetable plots. Society assigned to these women, idled by historical change, the task of shaping the future of their infants. A perfectly nurtured child who married well or mastered the skills that led to a position of prestige in the larger community would enhance the family's status. As the children of the bourgeoisie lost their economic value, they became investments in the family's future, and parents began to view them as objects of sentiment and pleasure.

* Another wonderful, and curiously soothing, treatment for parental worrying is to read books written by elder statesmen in the child development world. They invariably project a sense of calm, although sometimes a fatalistic calm, about children's outcomes. These elder statesmen are like mothers of several thousand children. They are big believers in the essential character of children—they say more and more often, as they get older, something that sounds like, "Kids are going to turn out the way they will turn out, so stop worrying about it." They also know that a great deal of how a child turns out is due to luck, which can be comforting for some parents and greatly disconcerting for some others.

To gain such a historical perspective, try the following thought experiment: Imagine that you meet someone who elevates one of the *other* household jobs to a special full-time status. Imagine that you meet someone who feels that buying and preparing food for the family is a full-time job; the person spends pretty much all his time preparing food, or thinking about how to prepare food better. He reads about food, talks to other cooks about where to get the best food, and most important, feels guilty and resentful about the time he is forced to do other things, because "preparing food is a full-time job." At night, he sometimes lies awake, tossing and turning because the lamb chops he served were a little overdone, or he heard that his favorite source for organic lettuce is going out of business. Where will he get lettuce now, he wonders disconsolately.

Although many of us do like to eat well and do spend a lot of time on it, if we met someone who made cooking for the family (or cleaning or laundry) a full-time job, we would think the person was oddly obsessed or unbalanced. But this might be precisely the judgment that traditional mothers in most of human history would make in watching people of our time think about children. Children are important, of course, such a mother might think, but not important enough to be a full-time job. She might have said, rightly, and possibly sadly, "I have too many other jobs to do."

"THE WORLD IS A DANGEROUS PLACE."

In the past, people somehow got by, and usually with a fair amount of substitute care. Most people in human history were not able to afford the notion that parenting is a full-time job, and they certainly couldn't afford the notion that looking after children could be done only by a child's own mother. Taking a historical view, there are many reasons for the rise of the emphasis, for most people, on the primacy of mothers (or parents) as caretakers. Kagan suggests several, including, for example, the influence on the culture at large of John Bowlby's attachment theory, which specifically addresses a child's tie to his own mother, and which may itself have been an historical reaction to the cruelties visited upon orphaned and refugee children during and after the Second World War.

What do mothers do that substitute caregivers do not? The answer to this question, I believe, lies at the root of a great deal of contemporary parental worrying. In the fantasies of parents who are contemplating substitute care for the first time, catastrophic thinking magnifies the import of the decision. "What if something happens?" parents say to me. "Like what?" I say, trying to push for the articulation of the unspoken fear. "If there were an emergency . . ." If there were an emergency, like a fire, or an explosion, or the intrusion of a deranged criminal, a substitute caregiver might save herself, or her own child, or another child first, *but a mother will always save her own child first.*

The reason mothers believe this is because it is true. Evolutionary psychology, and attachment theory before it, may suggest elegant explanations about the necessity of self-sacrifice depending upon the degree of relationship and the degree of shared genetic material, but mothers know one thing as an unshakable conviction: that if they were there in an emergency, they would save their own child first. This is a foundational belief of most humans I know, and I certainly do not believe that this belief will wither away anytime soon.

But the reason that this conviction is so important is that, as I hear so often from contemporary parents, "the world is a dangerous place." The often unspoken argument goes like this: "A child's mother is the only person who can absolutely be counted upon to sacrifice herself if the child's life is in danger, and these situations are happening with more and more frequency. The world is, increasingly, a dangerous place. Therefore, a child must be looked after by his mother, and no one else." In this unconscious but powerful logic, the more dangerous the world is, the more a child needs his or her own mother and no one else as a primary caregiver.

This logic makes sense, in a way, but the flaws are also obvious. The necessity of mother care *only* is in direct proportion to the perception of the world as a dangerous place. And the perception of the world as a dangerous place can be greatly affected by a number of other things, including, for example, too much exposure to contemporary media, in which the worst-case scenario is always the focus of attention (see Chapter 3). The perception of the world as a dangerous place can also be affected by a parent's own experience of trauma or danger as a child: the leap from "The world was a dangerous place for me" to "The world is now a dangerous place" is a very short one for many parents. As we have already noticed, the assumptions parents make about the more or less real safety of the world can be affected by all sorts of factors, many of them far from objective or rational.

THE HANDS OF STRANGERS

For many parents, the decision to pursue substitute care is bad enough. But once that hurdle has been got over and parents do decide they can deal with whatever it means to have a child looked after by a not-mother, a whole new set of problems appears. Even if the world is not seen as a dangerous place, there is one source of danger that is feared above all else: the substitute caregiver herself. If we didn't have enough to worry about, in terms of the effects on our children of being away from us, we also have to worry about caregivers. Many parents today lived through the day care sexual abuse scare of the 1980s, an epidemic that turned out to be grossly exaggerated. Public anxiety about sexual abuse in day care centers has largely abated, except in the unconscious or partially conscious fears of parents who lived through this agonizing period of time. And just for a booster shot, for those who were finally settling down about this issue, we had the Louise Woodward case in 1997, in which a British au pair was charged with killing an infant under her care by shaking the baby too hard. Every parent with a young child who lived through that period learned, all over again, that *when it comes to child care, you can't trust anyone but yourself.* (And if you must have substitute care, get a nannycam, because you certainly can't trust *them.*)

Beyond the worst-case worry of whether or not your child will actually physically survive substitute care, there is the question of the long-term effects of such care. What does it mean, for a child's long-term development, to be cared for by someone other than his mother? This question has been tossed around in academic circles for several decades, especially since the great wave of maternal employment outside the home that began in the 1970s. The research has shown, pretty unequivocally, that there are no long-term ill effects from a child being in group care if the quality of the care is sufficient. But the latent anxieties are still waiting to be set off, and can be pretty easily. As recently as the summer of 2001, the national news media were filled with reports that "day care makes children more aggressive," and the national community of parents set off on another round of agonized soul-searching. In fact, the findings that made the news were preliminary results released by one particular researcher before the study was concluded, and the meaning of the findings was much more equivocal and nuanced than the media reported. While it may be true that, in some measurement contexts, children who have been in group care are a little more insistent on getting their own needs met, it is not clear that (*a*) this is aggression or (*b*) this is a bad thing or (*c*) it is an effect that outlasts the context of measurement. In home care settings, children's needs are pretty well known to their parents or primary caregivers, and they probably do not need to ask or articulate their needs so clearly; the empathic adult looking after them knows what they want before they ask for it. Day care kids might need to be a little more pushy, since they are in a context in which it is less likely—not unlikely, but less likely—that the adults will know what they want before they ask for it. But this commonsense finding was brutally magnified in the press, and therefore in the minds of the reading public, who are already predisposed to believe that substitute care is harmful to children.

THE LOGIC OF SUBSTITUTE CARE

The harmfulness, or not, of substitute care is not a mystery. Indeed, one of the lasting, and often unsung, contributions of the feminism of the 1970s was the demystification of substitute care; there is not something magically nefarious going on when a child is not being looked after by his own mother. What these researchers pointed out is that, *if the caregiver has the qualities of a good parent,* substitute care is substantially similar (in terms of developmental effects) to being cared for by a parent. It is not identical; it does not feel the same, because the adult misses out on a lot and the child misses his or her primary caregiver. This sense of loss is important, indeed vital in some families. But research so far has not documented that there are long-term detrimental effects, in terms of cognitive or emotional development, for children who have been in substitute care.

The logic of substitute care, then, is relatively easy to understand. If we take what we know to be the characteristics of good parents, and use them to measure the quality of substitute care, we can begin to know whether or not children will have good parenting in such care. For example, we might assume that *experienced* substitute care providers who provide moderate firmness (see Chapter 2) in a context of empathy and a goodness of fit between a child's individual temperament and the demands of the situation will be good substitute care providers.

In assessing these characteristics in both parents and substitute caregivers, we might think about who possesses which of the important component attributes of parenting. One could argue that substitute caregivers, especially those who have been trained by schooling or long experience, will have the edge over parents in the moderate firmness category. Extremes of authoritarianism or permissiveness (that is, an extreme need to have a child knuckle under or an equally extreme need never to make a child unhappy) are most probably the result of personal idiosyncrasy anyway; people who have extreme opinions in this regard have usually had some kind of extreme experience themselves that is translated into dogmatic parenting ideology. We might also safely assume that a trained or experienced caregiver will have been affected by market forces, so that people who have excessive or extreme personal agendas will have been weeded out in training or by lack of success, failure to get good references, repeated firing, and the like. Caregivers with well-articulated but extreme philosophies of caregiving that are not a result of personal pathology—for example, those from religious or philosophical backgrounds who come with an outlandish set of tenets—can be identified pretty easily and avoided, if the goal is firmness in the context of moderation.

In thinking about goodness of fit, substitute caregivers may also have the edge over many contemporary parents. If we accept the hypothesis that more experience with a wider variety of children gives a person a better sense of which qualities in children are inborn and unmodifiable, the person who possesses that wider experience with many different children with different temperaments is likely to be the substitute caregiver. Substitute caregivers also have larger repertoires available to them to select their tools, so to speak, to fit the child. Again, experience here is the key: if substitute caregivers are better at finding a good fit between a child's temperament and the demands of the environment, it is only because they will have had a wider range of experience. Experience here does not mean age, or the experience of raising one child successfully; it means having seen and cared for a wide range of children with a wide range of temperaments, so that the caregiver will have had a chance to develop flexibility and wisdom.

It is in the realm of empathy, the ability and disposition to see the world from one child's point of view, that a child's parents will inevitably shine. In terms of information, parents who have been living with a child day in and day out since birth clearly have more information than a substitute caregiver to enable them to know a child in a genuine way. Talented substitute care providers can acquire this knowledge, but that takes time. And time with a child, that is, accumulated historical time, is one of the major factors that affects adequacy of substitute care. This is why any situation with a lot of turnover is bad for children; adults need time with children to get to know who they are, in order to be able to read what they need. The evaluation of how day care affects children, if high-turnover centers are counted in, is not a fair test. It is not "motherness" or "nonmotherness" that is at issue here; it is the amount of time available to develop a relationship with a child.

Thinking clearly about substitute care must also involve a consideration of the number of children being cared for at any one time. Let's assume that the fairest and most reasonable comparison is a one-to-one comparison: a child with his or her own mother, and no other children present, versus that same child with a nonparent adult who is comparable in terms of parenting skills and values, including moderate firmness, empathy, and goodness of fit. This would be the pure comparison of whether motherness or nonmotherness had any decisive impact upon a child's development. Comparing one-on-one with mother and one-on-many with a substitute caregiver is comparing apples and oranges, which is not always bad, but not always useful, either. And whatever you do, don't ask the child in this situation, because most children, even young children, get bored with too much sameness and, given a choice, will opt for the occasional, or even regular, empathic baby-sitter over the omnipresent mother.

But . . . about those oranges. In order for child care to make economic sense, in most cases it is done in a group setting. And in group settings, immediate attention to needs or wishes is not the rule. In most child care settings, even infant groups, children are asked to wait their turn. Children who are in day care settings before they are toilet trained sometimes have to wait to be changed longer than they would wait in a family setting, depending upon the size of the family. Children need to wait to eat, to go outside, to play with a favored toy; being in group substitute care is all about learning to wait.

One of the most fascinating things to observe in young children is the development of their ability to wait. Whether this is called impulse control, or delay of gratification, or increased attention span, the thing that children are doing is learning how to wait. Actually, this learning is largely accomplished by neurological development. As the brain matures, the ability to inhibit impulsive action grows throughout childhood, right on through adolescence. And within this large developmental progression, individual differences in the development of the ability to wait make for pretty wide variations within groups of children, especially during the early years.

Of course, these differences in waiting ability affect success in group experiences. In my consulting work I have observed this over and over: children who do not succeed in group care settings are very often children who have not yet developed, for developmental or personal historical reasons, an ability to wait that is in accord with the expectations of the group. One child I was observing demonstrated this very clearly to me when I was called in to observe yet another "meltdown day" in her three-year-old classroom. The children had helped their teacher bake cookies, and they were taking turns holding the platter out for a group of assembled grown-ups to take a cookie. The children were extremely proud and amused, of course, to be the feeders instead of the fed, so this was a highly valued activity. But my little problem child was flinging herself around so much, trying to push ahead in line and grab the plate, that I had to step out of my observer role and help the teachers out. I picked her up and carried her away a little distance and talked to her about what was going on. I finally said, "Your teacher said you were going to get a turn like everyone else. Do you believe her?" She looked at me somberly and said, "No. I never get a turn."

At three, of course, she was too young to be able to talk about *why* she didn't believe her teacher, or why she couldn't remember, at that moment, that she had ever had a turn (I know she had; I was there often enough to see her get a turn plenty of times). But the message was clear. We went back and asked the teacher again if she was going to get a turn; by that time, it was her turn, and so the temporary crisis was averted. Children like this, who for neurological or emotional reasons cannot wait as well as the others in their group, are the ones who need extra help if they are to thrive in group care.

Which is why child care settings have legal guidelines that mandate provider-to-child ratios. There is a minimum standard that corresponds roughly to the average child's ability to wait to have his or her needs met, and there cannot be any more children in the room than the guidelines allow, for precisely this reason. Children in group settings are beginning to be socialized, to conform their own needs to the needs of a community. That means learning to wait your turn, and the size of the community can increase as children's ability to wait increases with age.

Seen in this light, the decision, and the worrying, about whether a child can be in a group care setting is a decision about a child's ability to wait and a parent's wish to have them exercise this ability. In terms of parent versus nonparent care, the size of the group is a relevant, but not mysterious, issue. Children in larger families are always required to wait, even by their parents, but even most large families don't have three or four or more children all at the same developmental level (for most families, having four children does not mean having four children in diapers), so the abilities to wait are spread around a little. A child in a group of one or two, with a parent or a single substitute caregiver, will never have to wait as much, or at least as early in life, as a child in a group setting. This, again, is not about the mysteries of motherhood. This is about the age at which children and their parents are able and comfortable enough to begin the process of accommodating to a group.

And here is where values take over again. Being asked to wait, and beginning to be socialized, is a process of becoming aware that one is not special. Substitute care providers do their best to remind children that every child is special, and they certainly make efforts through celebration of birthdays and star days and show-and-tell days to make children feel that they are special at certain moments: group care is not all about deprivation. But it is an early introduction to the idea that one is not the center of the universe, as most children are when they are at home. Group care is not perfect; it is a compromise between competing priorities. When it is wonderful, it is really wonderful, and parents who worry about whether or not to put a child in group care should be aware of how many children there are who love to be there, because the organized stimulation more than makes up for the lack of always being number one. When it is not wonderful, it can be pretty sad, as when a child is too stressed out or tired or sick, and is looking and acting like a baby who needs the undivided attention of his mother—but she is still at work. But it most often works, and the surrender of our child's specialness probably has a lot to do with our own memories of feeling special or not special. Once again, this is a decision where more findings from the world of science will not help. We already know that children are not as special in a group as they are at home; it's axiomatic. For those parents who do have a choice in these matters, our decisions must be based on our own self-knowledge and our own values. When are we ready to have our child begin the process of socialization, the beginning of the hard knowledge that every child is not special in a group of children with competing needs? There are some facts in the matter that may help us decide, and then there are the fantasies.

There is no other area in the world of child development that is so laden with controversy as the readings or misreadings of research on substitute care. The accusations of bad faith on both sides of what social critic Cathy Young calls the "mommy wars" could fill several volumes, and the reader is best referred to other sources for a recounting of this dreary tale. That being said, the research shows about what we would expect from the foregoing discussion. Children who are in good substitute care do better, and children who are in longer hours of substitute care do slightly worse, and the children who are the least able to wait, that is, infants, do less well than older children. For example, the 1999 results of the Abecedarian Project, carried out jointly between researchers of the University of Alabama and the University of North Carolina at Chapel Hill, showed that children in a high-quality university-based day care center had higher test scores, higher school completion rates, and even a delay in the average age of first childbearing when compared with children in lesser-quality day care. These findings held up even for children who started in all-day, full-time day care at six weeks of age. The study demonstrated the effects of high-quality day care in that student-teacher ratios were low, beginning at three-to-one and ending up at seven-to-one, and staff turnover was low because the staff salaries were high.

The best-controlled large-scale study of substitute care has been carried out under the auspices of the National Institute of Child Health and Development. The NICHD Study of Early Child Care and Youth Development, a landmark series of studies often cited for its exemplary research methods, has demonstrated over the last several years that while substitute care is not uniformly good for children, it is pretty good or not so good depending upon predictable patterns of the quality and quantity of care. The study, begun in 1991, has followed 1,364 children in a racially and ethnically diverse sample roughly matching the U.S. population. Children in the study were followed in a variety of substitute care settings, including care by fathers, care by grandparents, home-based day care, and center day care. The findings of the study are voluminous, but in general, the study has demonstrated that quality of care, as defined by smaller group sizes and lower staff-to-child ratios, did indeed produce child care that was more sensitive, responsive, and stimulating, and that high quality of care was associated with better outcomes for children on measures of cognitive, language, and emotional development. The quality and amount of care were also related to differences in mother-child interactions: for example, higher amounts of child care during the first six months of life were associated with less maternal responsiveness at thirty-six months. Children who spent more hours in care in the first two years were higher on measures of caregiver-reported misbehavior, but these differences disappeared by the age of three.

The NICHD study has found, and will probably continue to find as it gathers data over the next several years, that sensitive interactions with children make a difference in their lives, no matter who is performing these sensitive interactions. It is also clear that substitute caregivers who are better trained and better paid are better at providing such interactions, and they are more likely to be able to do so if there are fewer children per adult in the substitute care setting. These findings make sense, and are quite probably generalizable over the entire range of child care situations: child care works out pretty well if the caregivers know what they are doing and aren't spread too thin. From the point of view of admirable social science methodology, one can only applaud the detail that has gone into this study, which uses the best tools of behavioral science and shows that substitute care is not harmful to children if it meets certain quality standards. On the other hand, one can only marvel at the weight of irrational worrying about substitute care, which suggests that this level of science needs to be brought to bear to demonstrate what ought to be pretty obvious: that child care is not magic. But it is the irrational stuff that drives the worry machine anyway: the fear of the substitute caregiver, who may harm your child no matter how benign she may appear.

SUBSTITUTE CARE:
WHAT THE NIGHTMARES SHOW

All this good research points out that, when it comes to substitute care, money talks. Low rates of turnover, good training, and caregiver satisfaction—all of these are expensive. Just as in regular schooling, lower adult-to-child ratios are the key to improvement, and also what costs the most. This is not irrational; it is about as rational as you can get.

But parents become irrational on the subject of money when it comes to substitute caregivers. Simply put, the more one pays for child care, the less sense it makes for a parent to work at all. Every parent knows this, but few parents are willing to discuss, or sometimes even admit to themselves, that they are looking to save a few bucks when it comes to substitute caregivers. Especially for people whose self-image is tied up with self-sacrifice, people who feel they would sacrifice anything or everything for their child, the money nexus is especially hard to bring to light.

Enter Louise Woodward. The au pair solution is a good example of some of the trade-offs parents are willing to make when it comes to caring for their children. Having an au pair— a young adult from a foreign country who lives in the home and gets, in payment for caregiving, room and board and the opportunity to experience the bounty and excitement of living in the United States—seems like a good arrangement. Parents get a caregiver whose attention is not divided (except between whatever children there are in the family) and the conviction that their child will still be special to the caregiver. The child will not be asked to wait, or be regimented, like children in group day care. And in-home care by an au pair is economically rea-sonable.

But. If a parent is looking for a good substitute caregiver, why would one choose someone who is, almost by definition, inexperienced? Au pairs have not, usually, had children, and they have often had some training, but not much. The mone-tary savings of having an inexperienced young adult caring for one's children is real, but the trade-off is that the experience and maturity that make for the best care is often lacking.

As a native of the American Midwest, I have often noted with some amusement and some sadness the inherent bad faith that goes into this bargain. Advertisements for live-in child care providers, domestic au pairs, appear regularly in newspapers in the Midwest, where girls with good, homespun Midwestern values are sought out to come and live in cities on the East or West Coast as in-home child care providers. The parents get low-cost in-home child care, and the young person gets to see the world and have room and board paid for. What could be better? The bad faith shows up in the inherent selection bias in these solicitations, whether within the country or from abroad. Young people, usually young women, who answer these ads are, presumably, the most adventurous of all their peers. The ones with the real homespun values will stay at home and raise their own siblings or their own babies. The ones who respond to the implicit promise to see the world might actually want to see the world, and therefore be *less* likely than their stay-at-home sis-ters to be content to devote their entire attention to caring for someone else's children.

The Woodward trial was a painful lesson in this reverse Darwinism. I have no opinion on the merits of the case—whether Woodward actually shook or abused the baby in her care, which resulted in his death. But the evidence brought forth at the trial was chilling: Woodward's interest in going out, exploring the city of Boston, and having fun with young people in nightspots on her nights off was introduced as evidence that she was not a devoted caregiver. It was pretty clear that Woodward was something of a party girl, but then, that is the bargain that goes along with au-pairdom: *you get to come to America and see the world.* Except, when you get here, you're not supposed to want to see the world, and evidence that you do want to see the world is evidence of scary irresponsibility, not befitting a child's caregiver.

The lack of trust between parent and caregiver—the source of much parental worrying—is very frequently displaced guilt about economic exploitation. What many parents cannot bear is this awful bargain: In order for working to make any economic sense at all, they must get a bargain on child care. But the bigger the bargain, the worse the economic exploitation. And the worse the economic exploitation, the greater the imagined aggression of the au pair toward their own child. Class warfare is the last thing one wants to introduce into a child care arrangement, and yet sometimes it is precisely what is introduced by the arrangements themselves.

Parents who are worried about substitute caregivers are often worried about whether the caregiver will love their child and make their child feel special. And they are sometimes even more worried about whether or not the substitute caregiver will hate or harm their child. These are the things that can give parents sleepless nights. But the hate enters into the fantasy when the parent feels, rightly or wrongly, that the caregiver is essentially being exploited. If that suspicion is present, it is almost impossible to sleep. Why wouldn't they hate the kids, if they hate the employers who are exploiting them? The treatment for this kind of worrying is simple to recommend, but difficult to follow: if a family wants to feel safe, they must enter into a relationship with a caregiver that does not feel like exploitation, because in child care, like in everything else, you get what you pay for.

✿   ✿   ✿

It is bound to keep parents awake at night if they imagine, for some of these reasons, that the person looking after their baby or child is bad, or mean, or sadistic. But then there's the reverse nightmare: what if the substitute caregiver is too good? What if my baby or child actually likes the substitute caregiver better than she likes me? Sometimes people who are insecure, and prone to feel unloved, cannot imagine that anyone else, including their baby, will love them either. For such a parent, a competent, experienced, wise baby-sitter is desired, and also deeply feared. This makes the whole thing ever so much harder; we want someone who will be good and attentive, but not too good. It's like trying to throw a baseball through a half-open window: it requires calculation, and luck, and it's really not easy. If you overcorrect too much in either direction, the results can be disastrous.

Most parents with this worry do not really appreciate how mythically important mothers are to their children. Adults in therapy who have been raised by substitute caregivers will always tell stories of loving nannies or baby-sitters who really made a difference in their lives, but almost never, in my experience, did they prefer the substitute. Mothers are just as important in children's mythic lives as children are in mothers'; there is something unique, undeniable, and primitive about children's connections to their real mothers, no matter how good the substitute caregiving is or has been.

POSTSCRIPT: BRUTAL FANTASIES, BRUTAL FACTS

To some readers, the foregoing discussion might seem a little, well, *hard.* Could it be that so much parental worrying about substitute care comes from such dark places: An unspoken wish to save money by skimping on caregiver costs? The insecurities and self-doubts that lead us to feel that, in a cuddly contest with a caregiver, we will surely lose? If these fantasies seem a little dark, how about the brutal facts in these matters?

The Centers for Disease Control put out a little publication called the "Weekly Morbidity and Mortality Report," which analyzes various trends in what makes all Americans unhealthy, or what kills us, and how. In the WMMR for March 8, 2002, the CDC reminded us that children are more likely to be murdered during the first year of life than at any other age until age seventeen. Most children who are killed in the first year of life are killed on the first day of life, and in approximately 90 percent of the cases, the perpetrators on record are the infants' mothers. (Although the CDC doesn't mention them, we can assume that a sizable portion of the remaining 10 percent might be the infants' fathers.) There is another spike in infant homicide around the age of six to eight weeks, which researchers have noted corresponds to the peak amount of crying time in most infants' lives.

The CDC also tells us that most mothers who kill their children are young and really scared, or mentally ill, or both. We can protect ourselves from worrying about our own children by telling ourselves that these people are monsters, a different species from us. Or we can tell ourselves that mothers or fathers who are alone on the job, who are isolated and stressed out, are sometimes in danger of losing it, no matter how much they love their children. These facts might help us to remember that a substitute caregiver is most often a preventer, not a perpetrator, of infanticide. The brutal truth is, substitute caregivers have saved far more lives than they have taken.

Try This at Home

1. If you haven't already done so, evaluate your child's substitute caregiver on the dimensions of moderation, empathy, and goodness of fit. If the caregiver has shortcomings, are they shortcomings you can live with?
2. Take a set of developmental milestones, like the first steps, the first smiles, or later developmental memories— the first day of school or chickenpox—and think about whether you can bear not to be there for them. If you would hate yourself for the rest of your life because

someone else taught your child to ride a bike, maybe you should reconsider substitute care.

3. Spend some time remembering your first experiences in groups, either in groups of siblings or in school. Do you remember what it felt like? If the transition from special baby to just another kid was too rapid or traumatic for you, try to imagine a way that it could be less rapid or traumatic, and therefore more survivable, for your child.

4. Imagine you are an attorney and try to put a dollar cost on pain and suffering. If getting child care at a bargain is making you worry a lot about your child, add the dollar cost of the worrying into the equation. Good child care is not cheap, but good child care helps you sleep better because you can feel more secure about your child's health and well-being.

5. Meditate upon the fact that children cannot choose their parents. This is a profound truth, but practically speaking, it means that they are stuck with you, in a unique relationship that transcends logic. If they sometimes like the baby-sitter better than they like you, try to remember that you will always win in the long run.

6. If you feel that the world is a dangerous place, and therefore your child needs to be with you at all times, make sure you have a support network anyway. The world can truly be a dangerous place for a child who is always alone with an isolated, stressed-out parent.

Six

DO AS I SAY,
NOT AS I DID

Jason's parents are pretty worried lately about their son and drugs. Their son is fourteen, a student in eighth grade. He has some difficulties keeping up with his schoolwork, and although he is well liked in school, he doesn't feel well liked. For some time he has been wearing clothes that seem outlandish or disrespectful to his relatively conservative, professional parents. He wants to wear clothes that are torn here and there; he wants to dye his hair blue; he wants to get his eyebrows pierced, although he hasn't done it yet. He is tattooing himself with a blue pen, and wants to get real tattoos as soon as possible. His parents suspect Jason has been drinking some of their liquor; they have found a pipe in his room, which he swears he is keeping for a friend. Sometimes he acts weird, and his parents think he might be high on something. They feel they are losing him, and they think drugs might be the cause of this behavior change.

This is the second time I have seen Jason. The first was more than a year ago, and when I meet with him again, I can understand why his parents are worried. He tells me, in the confidential setting of my office, about his recent experimentation with drugs. In seventh grade, he stole liquor from his parents, diluting their vodka and bourbon so they wouldn't know. He got so drunk he couldn't stand up, and threw up all over himself (he later told his parents he had a stomach flu). This year, he has been smoking marijuana on occasion, and he has started hanging around with kids at school who have also smoked marijuana. And just last week, he took a pill given to him by a friend: he was told it was ecstasy but he wasn't sure later; it just made him feel dizzy and spaced-out for several hours, but it wasn't as fun as he thought ecstasy is supposed to be.

Jason is clearly starting down a bad road. It might not be as bad as his parents think, and it might be worse. So far, this still qualifies as experimentation. But in talking to Jason, several things become clear: the change in his behavior predated the experimentation with drugs by at least a year. His wish to be shocking and unconventional, to look different from his classmates and to provoke a negative reaction from his teachers, came along at the end of sixth grade, almost a year before he ever drank liquor, and eighteen months before he tried pot. He spoke, back then, of his disgust for his classmates because they were so immature, by which he meant dependent on the good opinion of adults. He decided pretty early on that pleasing adults—doing well in school, looking the way adults want him to look, and hanging out with the right kids—is undesirable, and not pleasing adults is desirable because it makes him feel independent and mature.

Let's begin our understanding of this by stating the obvious: one problem is that Jason hates his parents. Well, he doesn't hate them exactly. What he is experiencing is a thorough rejection of the idea that parents, and by implication all adult authority figures, are helpful. For want of a better term, let's call this radical rebelliousness, and place it on the far end of the spectrum of adolescent expressions of independence. In Jason's case, the experimentation with drugs is clearly a symptom of, but not a cause of, radical rebelliousness. That's pretty clear in Jason's case because the rebelliousness came first, long before the drugs, as it frequently does.

Before we go on, a little caveat is in order. This discussion, about adolescents and drugs and authority, takes a particular path in a complicated cloverleaf of paths to understanding. It is relatively common, these days, to think about Americans' solutions to drug problems in terms of the *supply* side (how to limit access to drugs) and the *demand* side (how to limit the wish for drugs that makes people go into the drug business in the first place). The argument that follows is about the demand side, because that is, frankly, the side of interest to psychology. This is not to imply disrespect for the efforts of those who focus on the supply side. Clearly, limiting access to drugs is a vital part of a solution to limiting illegal drug consumption.

But adolescents will always have access to some kind of drug. Adolescents who are ready, willing, and maybe eager to use drugs will always be able to get their hands on something they're not supposed to have, and that's the real point: they want it because they are not supposed to have it. And the list of things they are not supposed to have is a long list—of things that are hard to make unavailable. The list includes alcohol, which most parents have; stimulant medications, which might be prescribed for a child or a child's friend; glue, cigarettes, cigars, chewing tobacco, and nicotine gum; and all the illegal drugs that somehow find their way into our communities. Most kids who are ready to take a drug are pretty indiscriminate about which one they take; they don't always start with one thing and move on to the next. They start by being ready to take drugs, and then take the first thing available.

This discussion is also not meant to downplay or ignore the addictive potential of many drugs. The AA maxim "First you take the drug, then the drug takes the drug, then the drug takes you" is a useful way of thinking about addiction. After a while (and sometimes, as in the case of nicotine, a pretty short while) the drug taking ceases to be experimentation and takes on its own independent life. In terms of treatment, this is important; therapeutic treatments for drug *addiction* that focus on the motivations for taking drugs and don't deal with the addiction part are pretty unsuccessful. The current wisdom, which I advocate completely, is that true addiction needs to be treated first, as addiction, before useful therapeutic work can be done on why you wanted to take drugs in the first place.

We can assume, then, that there is a population of kids who start using some drugs and end up using a lot of drugs, either because they are treating some untreated suffering by getting medicated any way they can, or because they have a particular biological vulnerability to addiction that has shortened the usually long road from experimentation to dependence. These problems are not new at all; the drugs of choice have changed somewhat, from alcohol in the fifties to marijuana and LSD and mushrooms in the sixties to cocaine in the seventies and eighties to ecstasy and Ritalin now. No matter what the drugs, this part of parenting has not changed. Kids with untreated mood disorders and kids with family histories of addiction are real worries, far beyond the scope of normal worrying that is our subject. If anything, things are somewhat better for these children now than they were in the past, because of increased sophistication about the possibility of self-medication for undiagnosed mood disorders.

But most kids who start experimenting with drugs are not yet addicts, and in thinking about them, we are thinking about the first part of the AA maxim: "First you take the drug." When we think about our children and drugs, it is useful to think about that state of being ready to take drugs. What brings that about? How do kids get to the place where, if they are offered a drug, they will take it, or will even go out and seek it? And how do contemporary parents react to, or facilitate, this decision?

Let's go back to that continuum of rebelliousness. Adolescents need to learn to think for themselves, and they need to make their own decisions. The development of the ability to make one's own decisions is a very long process, and there are usually some bumps in the road that make life difficult for everyone. Young adolescents are often oppositional; they decide to take their decisions into their own hands, but they have no idea what to do, so they decide to do the opposite of what their parents want. This kind of primitive oppositional behavior is usually not so dangerous, and frequently comical, because it is so pseudoindependent: trying to be independent, but having no idea what to do, a lot of kids just look at what Mom and Dad want them to do and do the other thing.

Later on, if things are going well, kids will decide they want to be independent by transferring their allegiance from parents to some other authority. This could be a coach, or a beloved teacher or pastor, or some other adult who inspires a teenager to emulate a temporary guru; a good example is the kid from a secular family who, as a result of a connection with an admired priest or rabbi, becomes much more observant than his family. These are the kids who change allegiances: talented skaters or skiers who decide, in high school, to give it all up in favor of being a pole-vaulter or a poet, usually as a result of a good connection with a nonfamily adult who serves as an avenue to independence from family influence. By changing allegiances, kids can still feel connected to an admired adult, but since it is not Mom or Dad, they can also feel independent from the family.

At the further, scarier end of this continuum is what I have called radical rebelliousness. This means a kid decides that all adult authority, and I mean *all* adult authority, is useless or harmful. This is beyond normal divergence. This is not the kid who decides to branch out and dye her hair green for fun, and gives it up very shortly thereafter with a fair amount of embarrassment. This is the kid for whom every manifestation of authority itself is seen as malevolent. Teachers are the enemy, so there is no point in doing well in school. Dress codes are challenged, not for the purpose of trying on a new self but for the purpose of being challenging. Supervised extracurricular activities are abandoned in favor of unsupervised extracurricular activities. Adults are experienced in a paranoid fashion as the source of all evil. In this context, experimentation with drugs is very common, almost inevitable, because it is such an easy and available way to express contempt for adult authority. Most kids in this situation are like Jason; their behavior does not change because of drugs, but their behavior changes are all occurring at the same time, and experimentation with drugs goes along for this particular ride because of the potent symbolic meaning of taking drugs.

The meaning of taking drugs is, for lots of adolescents, the act of breaking the law; for many kids, drugs are appealing, initially, not because they are fun but because they are a transgression. It is cool to use drugs precisely because it is against the law. At least since the time of James Dean, the original meaning of "cool" has been a public, romanticized, flagrant statement of one's outlaw status. "Cool" is now used as a general synonym for "admirable" or "desirable," as in a cool car or cell phone, but its original meaning was something more powerful and more aggressive—what the cultural critic Adam Gopnik has called "the accumulation of unembarrassed insolence that is known in America as cool." This is why, although I completely sympathize with the goals of drug education, I shudder when I hear grown-ups telling kids that "taking drugs is not cool." Since what "cool" means, especially to kids who are in this state of mind, is "illegal, flouting authority, not knuckling under to adults," then it makes no sense to kids to say that taking drugs is not cool. One can honestly say, "You don't really need to flout authority," or, "You can flout authority without taking drugs." That's all true, and maybe even useful. But saying, "Taking

drugs is not cool," is like saying, "Breaking the law is not breaking the law." It doesn't make any sense. It certainly doesn't
make sense to many teenagers I know.

PROBLEMS WITH AUTHORITY

When children are in this state of mind, their parents are pretty
worried. Being on the receiving end of the separation process
is hard enough—it's not unlike just plain old rejection to have
your child take off after some other beloved parent-type figure
and abandon the values, hopes, or standards that you have set
forth for her. But the closer a child gets to the scary end of the
continuum—the end where there are no grown-ups in sight—
the worse it is. The issue here is not drugs; drugs will be there
soon enough. But when a kid is in the no-adult zone, and seems
to be aggressively pursuing a truly no-adult zone in every
sphere of his life, the problem is not drugs. The problem is one
of cultural transmission itself.

Authority has, of course, many components, but one can
certainly recognize the simple positive component—I know
more than you do and I can teach you what I know—as well as
the simple negative component: I have more power than you
do and I can make you do what I want you to do. But when kids
are rapidly moving toward the rejection of both the positive and
the negative aspects of authority, they are in danger of using
drugs, as well as in danger of doing all sorts of things they are
not supposed to do. They become unteachable because they
are avoiding all manifestations of adult authority, both positive
and negative.

The problem is, where's the breakdown on our side, the
side of the supposed authorities? This is where it gets sticky for
many American adults, and depending on how old we are, a lot
more sticky for us than it was for our parents or for parents
in previous generations. In order to assert authority over our
children, we need to feel as if we are people who know some-

thing useful that we can impart to our children—that we know more than they do, and that they would be better off knowing what we know. We also need to recognize and be comfortable with the fact that we are people who have more power than they do and that we can and will and want to make them do things they might not want to do.

Youth worship is not particularly new in this country, although many have argued that it is now, because of the vast amounts of discretionary income that young people control, more florid than ever. If one is a television consumer, one can start to feel that kids are the only really important sector of the economy. Even though there are fewer of them, advertisers pursue younger consumers with a great deal of vigor because it is believed that they are people whose brand choices or identifications are not yet set in stone. Forty-five-year-old people are very unlikely to change their preferred brand of cola drink, but teenagers are still deciding. So advertisers pursue them relentlessly, and pursue them with advertisements with a pace and style that appeal to them—and that can leave adults feeling hopelessly uncool, or just plain old.

For more vulnerable adults, youth worship can translate into a premature sense of futility, as if the propaganda dished out to young consumers were really the truth, and adults didn't know anything worth knowing. Kids know more about computers than we do, so the story goes, and the innovative future that we all seek will be invented by them, any minute now. This version of the future is told with real gusto by some adults, especially those in the computer and entertainment industries; kids are not bound by rules, so they are better than we are—they are more *innovative*. And their comfort with breaking rules, with being innovative, leads to an inversion in the natural order of things: because they are not bound by old rules, kids show us the good new things, like cell phones with instant messaging capabilities—things that appeal mostly to kids but sell a lot of units.

I hope I will not be seen as anti-kid if I express something less than big-league enthusiasm for such innovations. One can make a lot of money following the kid-innovation thing; there are a lot of consumers for cutting-edge video games and cell phones with IM capabilities. So, while it is true that parents can get rich following the kids' innovations, many of us who are supposedly adults seem to have forgotten that what kids *in the absence of adult guidance* will invent is, very frequently, toys. Toys are good, no question. And if we want an all-toy-all-the-time world, we might be better off letting kids ignore us and go about their innovative activities unfettered by the kind of things we have to teach. But when we're looking for someone to cure AIDS or Alzheimer's disease, I'll stick with the kid who submitted to adult authority long enough to get through medical school, and then started to fool around.

Put another way, I am skeptical that the pace of technological change is so rapid that there must be a radical discontinuity between generations. While it is true that many adults I know are not as nimble around computers as their children, this is usually for two reasons: (1) they don't have the same amount of time to devote to the project, because they are working at something to pay the bills, and (2) they paid for the computer, so they are more worried that it will break, and they are therefore less likely to feel comfortable taking what appear to be risks with it. Adults who do have the time and mind-set to play with computers are perfectly computer literate, and this literacy can develop well into adulthood, because the tools that allow this literacy to develop—curiosity, confidence, and risk taking—are all qualities that develop outside of any particular application. There is no critical period for computer literacy; it is not the sole domain of the young, popular literature and humor to the contrary.

One of the things we need to do is to remember, to try to feel, that positive part of adult authority—that we have something important to impart to our children, even if commercial propaganda suggests otherwise. But the negative part of the authority question is much harder for most grown-ups than the positive part. That's the part in which we acknowledge that we have power and are ready to use it. By asserting the power of grown-ups, I do not mean power for its own sake, or the insistence on immediate compliance or blind obedience that characterizes the stance of the *authoritarian* parent (see Chapter 2). I mean the feeling of comfort that goes along with being an *authoritative* parent: that I know what is right, and I am comfortable enforcing a standard I know to be right, because *(a)* I am the adult, and *(b)* I know what adults are supposed to do, and most important *(c)* I like being an adult.

This is the hard part for parents of a certain age. For those who have come of age in any period since the 1960s, it is more than a little difficult to feel comfortable with authority. This is a knotty history, and is certainly not identical for every parent. But feeling like an authority, for people who were adolescents during or after the sixties, is experienced with the same unease that is felt by any successful revolutionaries when trying to assert authority after a revolution: there is always that whiff of ambivalence later on that makes it hard to stay in power.

YOU SAY YOU WANTED A REVOLUTION

Let's just take the year 1968, not because of its political significance, although the political events of that year (including the war, the mobilization against it, and the radical break between generations occasioned by the riots at the Democratic National Convention in Chicago) were pivotal psychological events in the development of everyone who was then under the age of twenty-five. I choose the year 1968 because one can point to that year as the year when adults caved in to kids. In the lifestyle revolution of the 1960s, 1968 was the first year when the adults said, "You're right and we're wrong." In the areas of both drugs and sex, adults who were in a position of authority largely gave up. Whether this was a good idea, or whose fault it was, is a very hot topic for some people, but is really irrelevant to the psychology of parenting. The point is that in many im-

portant ways the older generation, the parent generation of the time, pretty much gave in and acceded to demands of their children to remake the rules.

To give a brief example, consider the old notion of *parietals* in colleges. In women's dormitories there was a time, right up until about 1967, when young women were supervised in their college dorms. Young women could go other places to fool around with boys, and did, but the official policy was one that gave weight to the idea of restraint: men could visit girls' rooms only between two and four on Sunday afternoons, and when they did, there had to be at least one foot flat on the floor— rules that seem slightly ludicrous today. But these rules did say to young women (and these were women in *college*) that the adults would not permit or condone sexual activity, or at least not make it easy.

And then, in 1968, it was over. That was it. Rules changed overnight. Most colleges did away with parietals, and college students were free to do pretty much anything they wanted in their dormitories without adult supervision. Students' behavior had changed anyway, of course, but the rules held up by the adult authorities simply went away. I believe that under the historical circumstances of that time, it couldn't have happened any other way, but again, that is not the point. The point is that it happened, and the aftermath of such a precipitous defeat is part of the legacy of parenting today: parents now, even those who were not even born in 1968, have all grown up in a world in which adults' expectations for kids' behavior are tempered by the memories of what the adults were allowed to get away with in their own adolescence.

In my experience of parents who have grown up since those times, I do not see any sense of triumph or smugness about the escapades of youth. The simplistic view is that contemporary parents cannot uphold authority with their own children because they don't respect authority even now: the rap is, we can't ask our children to follow laws, because we were never too comfortable with laws to begin with. The reality of this, psycho-

logically, is a lot more complicated. For every adult I have known who covertly encourages his kids to break rules, I have known ten who cannot be authoritative because of the guilt and shame about what they were allowed to get away with in adolescence. There are a lot of contemporary parents whose attitude is, "Who am I to insist that my kid follow the rules? I battered my parents until they gave in, and therefore I don't deserve to pretend to be an authority."

PATHOLOGICAL INTEGRITY

Here's how the refrain goes: "I used drugs when I was his age, so how can I tell him not to?" Many parents try to do this, of course. They try to tell their kids not to take drugs. But they also, at the same time, covertly or not so covertly applaud any and every manifestation of antiauthoritarian behavior their children exhibit. They allow the hair dyeing and the body piercing, and they allow or support adult bashing of every kind. Kids are always going to break rules, the parents tell me—I know I did, and so why wouldn't they? And how can I insist that they follow adults' rules when I didn't? Doesn't that make me a hypocrite?

No. That doesn't make you a hypocrite. That makes you an adult. It is the job of adults to restrain the impulses of children. That's what adults are supposed to do. When our kids are adults, they will restrain their own impulses or not, but until then, our job is to restrain the excesses of youth. This is not to say we are perfect, and this is not to say that we can expect perfect compliance. But as we know in just about any law-enforcement context, enforcing laws has a way of making citizens understand that they are to be taken seriously. And not enforcing laws has a way of making people believe that laws are not to be taken seriously.

Many, many parents that I listen to are concerned about their own integrity; they feel that because they broke the laws when they were kids, they do not have the right to enforce

the law now. When I am feeling particularly grumpy about this aspect of contemporary parenting, I call this pathological integrity: the insistence on the continuity of the person above all else. There is, somehow, a feeling that "I am betraying myself and my youthful ideals if I act differently now than I did then." "When I was a kid, I believed that it was hypocritical for adults to drink and then tell kids they couldn't smoke pot. So now, when I say the same thing, I feel like a hypocrite . . . I feel like I am betraying myself."

Let's look at it the other way around: why is this continuity so important? For example, if one is not a priest, one cannot hear confessions; then, if one becomes a priest, one becomes a person who can hear confessions and prescribe penance. There is a lack of continuity between the two states, laity and priest; but people who are now priests do not usually feel hypocritical for hearing confessions because this is not consistent with their sense of themselves as a continuous person. They know they have changed into something else. The sense of the person can change, if we allow it to change, and we can feel comfortable acting in accord with the new privileges of the new person, without feeling that the behavioral inconsistency is an outrage against some notion of personal integrity. Adults are supposed to do the adult thing when they are adults, no matter what they did when they were kids. Insisting on personal continuity, or an overdeveloped concern about hypocrisy, may simply be a cover for a deep wish to remain adolescent.

This view of parenting adolescents is not new. There is a long tradition, in psychoanalytic theory at least, in which adolescents' acting out is often explained as children's acting out the covert adolescent wishes of parents. This older psychological literature points out the sometimes not-too-subtle way that parents instruct their kids to break rules. When a kid comes in late, a parent might say, "I know where you've been. I know you've been waiting until I go to sleep and then sneaking out and going down to that secluded place by the lake where the police never go, and I know you've been getting beer from that

liquor store on South Main where all the kids go to buy illegally, and I know . . ." By the time the parent is done with this speech, the kid knows the entire program, and the instruction manual is complete in every detail. Psychoanalysts have discussed this for decades, but it used to be seen as a relatively isolated pathology associated with parents who were covert lawbreakers—in an era when lawbreakers were few and far between.

A more contemporary version of this phenomenon is expressed in our own little information problem: What do we tell our children about our own drug use as adolescents? When they look us right in the eye and ask, "Well, did you use pot when you were my age?" what are you supposed to say? Many parents ask me this question with anguish, because they do not wish to lie to their children; many parents pride themselves on *never* lying to their children, although I am not sure it is possible to be a good parent and to take this particular vow.

In this situation, I frequently give parents the following exercise: Imagine your teenager says to you, "I heard some funny noises coming from your room last night. Were you and Mom having sex?" What would you say? Would you say *(a)* "Yes," because you never want to lie to your children? Would you say *(b)* "No," because it makes you uncomfortable? Or would you say *(c)* "None of your business!"? Although I am loath to boss parents around, they figure out pretty quickly that the right answer, at least in my book, is *(c)*. And most parents get the right answer; they are comfortable with some areas of adult life being off-limits to kids. They feel, I'm not going to lie, because I don't have to . . . I don't have to talk about this with you at all. It's an aspect of my life that I don't share.

So why can't our own lawbreaking, if there was any, be the same way? If a child asks, "Didn't you smoke pot when you were my age?" the answer could be, "That's none of your business. That's irrelevant. Many kids break the law when they are kids, because they don't understand how important it is to obey the law. But now I do understand that—and you need to under-

stand it too." Some people feel that kids will hear this and understand that this means "yes." But what is more important is that kids hear this and understand something about boundaries; there is a boundary between kids and adults that is a good thing—kids and adults are not the same in all ways.

This is, after all, another way of enacting the parenting principle of goodness of fit (see Chapter 2). The idea of goodness of fit implies a respect for children's inborn temperament, and an adaptation to, *but not a complete capitulation to,* the child's behavioral style, which is guided by that temperament. So it is with the negotiations between parents and kids about the law; we can expect that there will be some challenging of authority, which is natural to being a teenager, but we do not need to be so adaptive that we say, in effect, "I know you're a kid and therefore I can't expect you to follow the law." What we can do is to proceed with the expectation that kids will follow the law, and it is our job to identify with the law and enforce it, not harshly but firmly. While we do not expect complete robotic compliance from teenagers, we also do not give up on our own identification with the way people are supposed to behave.

And if we are uncomfortable with compliant kids, we need to examine that as well. The atmosphere of rebelliousness, and the enshrinement of "attitude," is so pervasive in our lives that most parents do not even notice the mixed messages they are sending. When parents deride kids other than their own because they are too good, or too compliant, or too law-abiding, what do they expect their own kids to hear? That kids are supposed to display some attitude? That kids who follow the rules are too nerdy to live? That in order for Mom and Dad to really love me, I need to break some rules, so they don't display the same contempt for me that they display toward those kids who they think are too good?

While it is counterproductive, parents' desperation in this department is completely understandable. It is already awfully difficult to feel satisfied with being an adult in an atmosphere that worships youth, and in which youth is synonymous with breaking the rules. There are some instances in which it is actually pathetic to see adults still trying to act like outrageous kids; for those who want to feel genuinely embarrassed, try reading the American Association of Retired Persons magazine that is designed to appeal to baby boomers, *My Generation.* Or if you really want to get depressed, watch any current performance by Mick Jagger. Mick teaches us one thing only at this point: for anyone over twenty-five, it is a short step from subversive to ridiculous, and that step gets shorter and shorter with each passing year.

It is the job of parents to act like adults, and one of the things that adults do is to uphold and respect the law. That may be harder for contemporary parents, because of the power of a culture that worships youth, and because of our own personal histories as adolescent rule breakers. But parenting demands something more of us than personal continuity, disguised as integrity; it demands of us that we accept a categorical break with childhood, and an acceptance of the role of parent, which is discontinuous with the role of the adolescent. When people say, "Being a parent is harder today than it has ever been," maybe one of the things they are saying is, "Being an adult is harder today than it has ever been." As a therapist who listens to both children and adults, I believe that this is one of the things people now say that happens to be true.

Parents who worry about their children experimenting with drugs are certainly right to be worrying, and children with an untreated emotional disturbance or underlying vulnerability to substance abuse are really the ones who need the most care. With the rest of our children, keeping them away from drugs or people who use drugs is a laudable goal, although probably completely unrealistic, due to the prevalence and easy availability of mind-altering substances. Kids don't turn to drugs unless, or until, they have already turned away from adult authority. As parents, we can examine how we contribute to that process—the ways, sometimes conscious, sometimes not, that we participate in saying that adult authority is not legitimate, or that adults aren't really worth listening to. Since this is a message kids are already primed to hear, it is pretty important for us to listen a little harder to ourselves to try to hear the bulletins we are sending out.

ADULT AUTHORITY:
THE FANTASIES

A good therapeutic way, then, of understanding many parental worries about children's drug use is to understand that these worries are a displacement from something else that is harder to talk about, harder to understand, harder to feel. Why should it be so hard to feel? It's not really that hard to think about breaking the rules, or to feel, consciously, uncool as an adult laying down the law. What may make it harder to think about, or feel, is the sadness involved in intergenerational warfare, including the intergenerational warfare in our own histories.

The best text for understanding this problem, and feeling the powerful sadness that underlies the problem of adult authority, is the book-length essay by George W. S. Trow, originally published in the *New Yorker*, entitled *Within the Context of No Context*. Trow's essay, which is a magnificent piece of writing, ends with a meditation upon the subject of his father's fedora. Trow thinks about this kind of hat, which was worn with conviction by his father and his father's father, and he sadly describes his father's conviction that Trow would also, one day, become a fedora-wearing adult. And then, at some point, the whole system went off the rails. Trow cannot wear this fedora in a straightforward way; he can wear it with irony, or camp, or self-mocking irreverence, but he cannot wear it with the conviction that adult men wear fedoras because that's what adult men do . . . to know they are men, to know they are respectable, to know they are adults. The beauty in Trow's account is that it is not an account of triumph; it is not an unmixed victory of sassy, proud youth over musty, constricted age. It is the sadness that goes along with the feeling that your father doesn't have anything to teach you, and therefore you don't have a father. And you have nothing to teach a son.

While this is never completely true, our daily lives give us plenty of data to suggest it is true enough. We don't wear fedoras anymore, and although businessmen still wear business suits, the pressure always seems to be in the other direction—think of the lionization of the blue-jeans-wearing entrepreneurs of the "new economy" of the 1990s. The return to respect for authority occasioned by the events of September 11 is still relatively new, and it remains to be seen whether this is a larger cultural trend or a blip that will fade away when everyone feels safe again. It has been fifty years since figures of authority, in the form of police and firefighters and soldiers, have been as publicly revered as they are now. It would certainly be a salutary development to see American parents jumping on this bandwagon and feeling less ambivalent about being authoritative themselves, but it is too soon to tell. A few short months after the terrorist attacks and the beginning of the war in Afghanistan, we also had the 2002 Olympics, during which the American press fawned over "extreme" athletes with lots of attitude (and open contempt for the Olympic rules about the use of illegal drugs), while simultaneously deriding musty old downhill and cross-country skiers, who do the same old thing they have been doing for a hundred years.

My number-one pick for the most prevalent unconscious, or simply unspoken, fantasy about authority is the following: "I defeated my father, so I don't deserve also to defeat my son." This, after all, would go against all our primitive notions of the symmetry of justice; in the Oedipus myth, Oedipus killed his father and was eventually exiled, because his offense against the natural order could not be allowed to stand. Those among us who feel they got away with defeating their own fathers (which is a lot of people) do not usually carry on in a wave of triumph and glory. They usually feel guilty and expect retribution, and what more fitting retribution could there be than defeat by our own sons? If we joined battle with our sons by insisting that even though we broke the laws and got away with it, they should follow the laws, isn't that kind of unfair?

Yes, it's unfair. But let's look at the corollary to this fantasy, the corollary Trow's work suggests: "My father gave up on me (by not insisting that I follow the law), and that really hurt. So why should I be a father to my son, when I didn't have a father of my own? Why should he get one when I didn't?" Stating the fantasy in this way reminds us that kids really want to be protected by the law, and even though they insist that they don't, they really want to have someone help them follow the rules. Insisting on the law, and insisting that adults really do have something to teach kids, is an act of love—*and kids know that.*

What we can do to stop worrying so much about our kids and drugs is to examine our own attitude toward authority. Do we think we are uncool, and are we heartbroken about it? Do we like being adults, and convey to our kids that adults are, in general, people who they should respect? Do we like to use illegal drugs ourselves, or like to break the law in other ways now? Being a good parent to an adolescent means giving up the fantasy of being a kid, but on the positive side, it means embracing the role and the activities of adulthood. If we can learn to love being adults, we can sleep better at night knowing that someone responsible is in charge—us.

TEENAGERS AND DRUGS:
JUST THE FACTS

In looking at the worst-case worries about kids and drugs, we do have access to a fair number of facts to use in trying to make reasonable probability estimations. This is another area fraught with statistical deceit, because advocacy groups that wish to demonstrate a huge problem or a huge lack of a problem use statistics in ways designed to persuade first and illuminate second. But here are a few facts, which can be read as demonstrating either a huge problem or, possibly, a trend toward progress.

Every year, the U.S. government funds the Monitoring the Future study, which is a nationwide survey of drug use by high school students. The study is carried out by the University of Michigan's Institute for Social Research and sponsored by the National Institute on Drug Abuse, an arm of the National Institutes of Health. The study has surveyed twelfth-graders every year since 1975, and added eighth- and tenth-graders in 1991.

The result of the Monitoring the Future survey in December 2001 demonstrated a continuation of the slight downward drift in drug use among high school students that has been going on for several years. In this survey, the overall downward movement was caused by a significant decline in the use of heroin among tenth- and twelfth-graders and a decline in the use of inhalants, with a significant decline in this category among twelfth-graders. The only drug that showed increased usage was MDMA (ecstasy), but the NIDA study showed the rate of increase in this category appears to have slowed in the study year.

As the study indicated, drug use among eighth-graders is lower than their recent peak year of 1996, while it continues among tenth- and twelfth-graders at about the same levels of the recent peak year, 1997. All of these levels are significantly lower than the twenty-seven-year all-time champion peak years in—guess when?—the late 1970s and early 1980s.

The rates of drug use vary, of course, by drug. For example, rates of self-reported marijuana use at least once during the past year were 15.7 percent for eighth-graders, 32.7 percent for tenth-graders, and 37 percent for twelfth-graders, compared to the all-time high of 50.8 percent of past-year marijuana use among twelfth-graders in the study year 1979. For heroin, the past-year rate for twelfth-graders is 0.9 percent (that is, nine-tenths of 1 percent of students reported using heroin at least once during the study year). This is the lowest rate since 1994.

The worst-case worries might also be captured in statistics on drug addiction, numbers that are very different from those for drug experimentation. Drug addiction rates would, of course, be expected to approximate the rates of drug addiction in the adult population as the average age of the adolescent sample approaches adulthood. For example, in a 1994 survey that drew upon data from a national survey of psychiatric diagnoses, addiction estimates for a population of adolescents and young adults (ages fifteen to twenty-four) were given as follows: the prevalence of substance dependence in the survey population was 13.6 percent for alcohol, 5.6 percent for cannabis, 2.6 percent for cocaine, 1.6 percent for stimulants, and 0.7 percent for hallucinogens.

What one makes of these facts is, of course, dependent upon the worry state of the parent involved. If one sees the world through the lenses of zero tolerance, then any of these numbers are too high. But if one looks at these rates with an eye toward reality-based probability estimation, the rates seem low enough. Of the 37 percent or so of high school seniors who have tried marijuana, about 5.5 percent become dependent upon this substance. These populations include the high-risk categories of children who have a parent with a substance abuse disorder and children with an untreated mood or other psychiatric disorder. Children and adolescents in mental health treatment settings are estimated to have substance use disorders in the range of approximately 50 percent. We can assume, then, that rates for the entire population, which contains these higher-risk groups, should be inflated by their inclusion, and lowered when children in these groups are excluded.

The message, at least the message I usually give out, is that the kids who really need worrying about are the kids in these two groups: those who are exposed through modeling and social influence to addiction through observation of their parents' addiction, and those who need treatment for an emotional disorder and are not getting treatment in conventional ways. Other kids may use drugs in other ways, not the least of which is an effort to defy authority and to be cool, which will go away gradually when the need to defy authority abates. This will happen either because the child has established him- or herself as separate, and feels separate, and therefore does not feel the need to throw off the oppressive yoke of Mom and Dad so strongly, or because the child has assumed the mantle of authority by having children—and many casual drug users do not stop completely until they have children of their own. Some people with children do not stop taking drugs, but presumably they settle into a pattern of adult drug use—legal social drinking, disreputable cigarette smoking, illegal pot smoking, or other varieties of drug use with which we as adults are all familiar—and they try as best they can to conceal this drug use from their children. Whether or not they succeed is a different story.

❖   ❖   ❖

As I have argued, drug use is often not what it seems. In many instances, experimentation with drugs is a feature of the separation process, and it is part of a wide array of things kids do to express their wishes to feel mature by not doing what grownups require of them. This is all familiar—we all went through it, and survived, more or less, although the process is rockier for some than for others. It is always better when it is gradual—from the influence of parents to that of nonparent adults and then peers, rather than from the influence of parents directly to that of peers. When parents see the latter version, they can make some real efforts to slow down or divert the process—by reaching out to their own kids or by trying to find some nonfamily adults who can have some influence.

The peculiar contemporary twist on this is the role of cultural transmission. The onslaught of kids' separation issues, when expressed as withering contempt for the world of grown-ups, is bad enough. But to survive it, a parent needs some reserves of positive feeling about authority itself and about him- or herself as an authority. If we feel we don't deserve to be authorities, for our own historical reasons, or if we feel that no contemporary adults deserve to be authorities, because we don't really know what our children need to know so we don't have anything to teach them, then we're in trouble when they hit adolescence. When that happens, it's time to put on that fedora and take a good long look in the mirror—and try like hell to figure out a way to like what you see.

Try This at Home

1. Think of an ideal separation process as one marked by a gradual movement away from the influence of parents. Now do a thorough inventory of your own separation from adult influence and your own experimentation with adulthood. Was it too sudden, or too gradual? Was it too early, or too late? If your own experience wasn't perfect, think about whether you try to correct or overcorrect for these imperfections in your own children's experience of adolescence.

2. Try to remember what your father or mother had to teach you in adolescence. Try to remember if there were things that you wished they would teach you that they did not.

3. If you don't know how to program your VCR, or how to run the computer you own, learn how—but not from your own child. Learn from another adult.

4. Ask yourself, are you cool? Is there an adult way you can experience being cool, without subverting your own authority? Helpful hint: if you are over forty, getting an earring (if male) or a tattoo isn't it; think of something else.

5. How about trying to be inventive without being transgressive? Can't you think outside the box without trashing the box? Practices that enhance creativity, like acting

or poetry classes, can help you feel young, and innovative, and even transgressive, and you can still uphold the law.

6. Practice saying, "None of your business," until you can say it nicely, so it doesn't sound mean, just discreet.
7. Think about giving your child, for his or her twenty-fifth birthday but not before, a complete account of your adolescence. It might be fun for you to tell them, after they are pretty much all grown up.

Seven

WHO'S AFRAID
OF THE BIG BAD
CULTURE?

A mother approaches me after a lecture. Her son has sworn at another child at school, and he was overheard by a teacher. The school has been very clear in letting her know that this is against school policy, and her son has had to go to detention, which has never happened to him before in his life. "We don't use that kind of language," she says. "I know people get frustrated, but we have been so careful." She looks to be in her early forties, clearly very worried about the fate of her eleven-year-old son. I keep listening. Although I think I know the answer to this one, I want to hear more about the identity of the culprit, the instigator, the person or agent who has turned her sweet son into a monster. "We're very careful about what he's allowed to watch on television, and he never goes to PG-13 movies. All I can think of is, it must be the music." The music? "I think he has a friend who listens to Eminem, and I think he made a copy of an Eminem CD of his own. I think that must be where he got the idea—he got it from the culture."

I knew this was coming, but I felt I had to check. I am always interested in the metaphors parents use to describe their parenting worries, and the infection metaphor is one of my favorites. Since contamination anxiety is as old as time, it is a metaphor that carries a lot of weight. But what is important about the infection metaphor here is not that the child is being attacked by invisible forces, but by *foreign* forces. The home is the clean, protected body, and the culture (made more scary by associations from the laboratory—the location of "cultures" of bacteria and viruses) is described as the foreign enemy that infects the child.

What is striking about this to me, and what seems to be new, is this aspect of parents' relation with (for want of a better phrase) the media culture. "Media culture" refers to a lot of stuff: television, movies, radio, the Internet, video games, print media. It's a pretty big media world, and, of course, each of these forms of media has specific manifestations and specific appeals. They also have specific effects on children and adults, which probably have more to do with their form than their content (more on this below). But these specific entities are lumped together in a term that suggests that parents experience them as all the same, a manifestation of foreignness or otherness.

If the media culture is an enemy presence from which we must protect ourselves, where does it come from? Who is sending it to infect our children? Parents all over the world protest the deleterious effect of American media; even before the terrorist attacks of September 11, 2001, the concept of "jihad versus McWorld" had entered the world of ideas as a way to describe the conflict that results when people seek to safeguard their traditions and their authority over their children against the onslaught of American values as carried in American media. It would make sense if one were, say, a Tibetan or Yemeni parent, to feel that American media culture is a foreign agent infecting the pure domestic culture of the home country, because America is, to them, a foreign country.

But why do Americans feel so invaded by their own cultural products? This is *our* stuff, as is so amply demonstrated every time we turn on the television. It is also continuous with stuff we, as parents, remember, and if we remember our history, we might also remember the history of the foreign infection metaphor. Rock and roll was, in its early days, seen as a subversive force; and as a subversive force, it was sometimes seen as a plot foisted upon America by our foreign enemies. In a sense, the paranoids of the day were right (at least more right than we are) because their sense of the foreignness or strangeness of rock and roll could be seen as the inevitable reaction of insulated white Americans coming up against the cultural products of African Americans.

But why, now, do so many parents feel that the culture is not us? If they are not *our* values, whose are they? Cultural conservatives have described this villain in personified form as "Hollywood": Hollywood is a community whose values are different from ours, and therefore the cultural products our children are exposed to are, in some important sense, foreign. The fact that these products sell so well belies the foreignness of them, and the question about the otherness of a community that is made up of expatriates from every corner of the American heartland is questionable, but the theme resonates well with many American parents. We all know that Elvis and Janis Joplin and Kurt Cobain were relatively harmless homemade products (and most parents who hate popular music for their children will happily allow them to listen to oldies or classic rock stations playing the music of outdated subversives), but Eminem or Lil' Kim seem to have been designed by Someone Else to seduce our children. This someone else is pretty powerful—we just don't know who it is.

VIVIDNESS AND THEATRICALITY
IN CHILDREN'S LIVES

Part of the reason that parents are worried about children's exposure to contemporary media is that it seems more powerful than the media we grew up with. It is more encompassing, more real, more engrossing, because it is more like life: in every sense, *it leaves less to the imagination.* The difference between a *Spider-Man* comic in the newspaper or on the newsstand and *Spider-Man: The Movie* is extreme. *Spider-Man: The Movie* is nothing if not vivid; it seems like everything is really happening on the screen, thanks to breathtaking special effects that are now a staple of contemporary television and movies. What has changed since we were children is precisely the vividness of contemporary media. And vividness is what begets imitation.

Imitation has been a subject of interest to psychologists for as long as psychology has been in business. For behaviorist psychologists, imitation was always a hot topic because of its contribution to children performing socially approved behavior. Developmental psychologists, led by the efforts of Jean Piaget in the 1930s, have always been interested in imitation as a way of knowing. Children imitate as one way, among many, of attempting to understand what is going on in the world around them. In this view, imitation is a way of understanding things that are not already understood, the things that stand out from the background of everyday life. Children imitate things that are vivid, so that they can understand what those things are like by feeling what it is like to do them.

To young children everything is new, and young children imitate lots of things in their play that are relatively mundane. Little boys and little girls imitate their father shaving, or their mother putting on makeup. Imitation is a way of understanding by experiencing what it feels like to do it; and there are some things, the things that seem odd or out of the ordinary, that children can best understand through imitation.

But once something loses its strangeness, it loses its power as an object of imitation. By the time children are five or six, they have stopped imitating their parents doing everyday things; everyday adult things are, by then, also everyday things for kids. It is the new, odd, and especially vivid things that retain their power as objects of imitation. Children of the fifties *played at* flying, in the way that children have always played at flying so they can know what it feels like to be a bird. But children of the fifties *imitated* flying after seeing two very strange things: Superman flying on television and Mary Martin flying onstage or on television as Peter Pan. Then kids really started flying: the vividness of the image, its strangeness, made it harder to understand in conventional ways—and therefore it had to be imitated to be understood. Of course, imitation is an incomplete way of understanding, and nobody really knows what it feels like to be Superman, even when they imitate him taking off, but it helps. It's one piece of the knowledge equation.

Seen in this light, it makes sense that parents are worried about contemporary media culture. It is precisely the vividness, or the strangeness, of it that is new, or at least different than when current parents were children. I believe that it is this strangeness that gives it both its sense of foreignness and its power. Children want to imitate the unusually vivid images, motions, actions that they see in the movies or on television, and the vividness of contemporary media comes from just that combination of lifelike and unlifelike that contemporary special effects provide. When Keanu Reeves bends in half to dodge bullets in slow motion in *The Matrix* it looks real, but it looks like an unreal thing really happening. When the martial artists in *Crouching Tiger, Hidden Dragon* fly around the trees, it looks both so real and so strange that it is captivating in its vividness: this is precisely the kind of visual image that children will imitate as a way of trying to understand. Anyone who has watched children or adolescents getting together after having seen *The Matrix* will understand this point; there are certain images, actions, or poses that are imitated again and again, as if the entire huge child population were on instant replay.

To return to our original example, it may be true that our likable, innocent eleven-year-old who gets into trouble for swearing at school is, in fact, doing so because of his exposure to Eminem. Very likely. Is it something to worry about? Probably not. First of all, if his parents make the mistake of thinking that this momentary imitation is the beginning of a road to perdition, they are not understanding the process of imitation. It is completely understandable why, after hearing Eminem or especially seeing an Eminem video, a kid would want to try that out to see how it feels. They might want to feel the power and strangeness that comes with unrestrained use of language: to say, "Fuck you," in public, or to scream it, or to scream it over and over, to see what that feels like. But after having done that, and felt it, most kids do not need to do it over and over; it is by definition a self-limiting phenomenon.

It is also the case that kids who have been very protected from the extremes of contemporary media culture might be more vulnerable to temporary imitation, because it is for those kids that the images are the most vivid and strange, for they have seen so few of them. Many parents who have been extremely cautious about allowing their children to be exposed to trashy movies or videos are utterly dismayed about their children's adolescence; at the point when children's access to media can no longer be effectively controlled by parents, the protected child who has never seen an image of a gun or heard an expletive will sometimes very quickly degenerate into, well, a degenerate, in the eyes of his or her parents. But these children have a lot of catching up to do. They want to know what it feels like to do all those things that are powerful, not because they have been forbidden but simply because they are new and strange. From the outside, this can sometimes look like a wholesale personality change, to be laid at the door of the media culture.

If you watch children closely, there is one thing you will never see: children imitating an action they have read in a book. Young children will imitate the voice of a beloved adult reading a favorite passage or word, like the voice Mommy makes when she reads the queen's words from *Snow White,* "Mirror, mirror, on the wall," which Mommy usually reads in a different voice from her normal reading voice. But when children learn to read to themselves, they almost never imitate a specific action they read in a book. They might play out a scene; they might take a chopstick and pretend to be Harry Potter saying an incantation; but it is not like imitating something that the child has seen or heard someone else do. The imaginal work has been done in the act of reading; in order to make sense in reading, a child needs to picture the action, and in performing that act, she has already come to some understanding of the act. The act has already been performed in the act of reading, so it doesn't need to be imitated again to be understood.

And herein lies the problem. There is a powerful connection between imitation and passivity. Images that are both very vivid and passively experienced are the things that children do imitate, in some sense *need* to imitate, in order to understand them. This is why the argument made by some cultural liberals, that censorship of media images makes no sense because contemporary television or movies are no more violent than, say, the Bible, is an argument that does not hold water. If a movie were made of the Christian Bible, using contemporary special-effects technology to portray as graphically as possible some of the more violent passages in the Bible (the slaughter of the firstborn children by King Herod, for example), there would be the same outcry about this movie as there is about any other terrifying violent movie—at least from me. Reading is not experienced passively, but television and movies are, and that makes all the difference.

In this context, parents are onto something when they

worry about the *escalating* quality of media outlandishness. Children who are on a steady diet of television or violent or mesmerizing movies will need the pace and the stimulation of these movies to escalate, in order to keep their attention. Even if the content is not at all violent, it is sometimes startling to watch television that is aimed at children and adolescents, to observe the pace and the overstimulation that is the current standard. Advertisements aimed at kids are jacked up to a degree that is unfathomable for most adults. Music videos are pretty much the same; the rate of change of the visual images is pretty remarkable, and videos that hold one image or camera angle for any length of time are just too slow-paced for most kids to find interesting. When parents talk about escalation, I believe that they are talking about the escalating pace of entertainment for children, which is independent of content but is still, somehow, disturbing.

Just try this little experiment: try watching an old movie with a teenager. Not too long ago, I happened to watch a pretty violent movie, Alfred Hitchcock's *The Birds*, with some well-modulated, not particularly jumpy teenagers. Seen through their eyes, at least as I understood their comments, the movie was completely unwatchable. It helps that it is in color (most kids now living will simply not tolerate anything in black-and-white) but the exposition is, well, leisurely. The setup, in which the character played by Tippi Hedren bumps into the character played by Rod Taylor in a pet shop and then buys a pair of lovebirds to deliver to his country home as a practical joke, was, for my teenage companions, excruciatingly slow. They could not sit for it; they left. Indeed, the first scary, outlandish thing that happens in this movie happens over a half hour into the movie, and the really scary stuff doesn't start until the movie has been going for well over an hour. It is a movie that was thrilling, even to teenagers, when it was first made, in 1963, but today would never be made at all (except possibly for PBS, the only venue in which slow-paced entertainment is still tolerated, and only because the average PBS viewer is so old).

PASSIVITY AND PACING

What television researchers have known for a long time is that content is not the only problem in assessing contemporary media. The problem with contemporary media, especially television, movies, and music videos, is that passively consuming fast-paced images is itself detrimental to children. This was amply demonstrated years ago by Jerome and Dorothy Singer of Yale University, pioneers in television research who were consultants to the development of *Sesame Street* back in the good old days when people had high hopes for children's television. The Singers discovered, through careful research on the effects of television on children's expressions of aggression, that rapid pacing itself has the effect of stimulating aggression in children, *independent of content*. It doesn't matter if a child is watching a fast-paced, sprightly demonstration of the daily activities of the letter *B* or a movie like *Natural Born Killers* (although, of course, the Singers did not actually use such a movie in their research). What they discovered was that the fast-paced cutting back and forth between television images was itself a problem: children who watched fast-paced television programs were more likely to be jumpy and restless after exposure to such programming, and more likely to engage in some form of aggression. As a result of the Singers' research, *Sesame Street* was slowed down, so that it would not do more harm than good while teaching children about the activities of the letter *B*.

This quaint concern for not overstimulating children has not been heeded in the development of contemporary programming. Indeed, programming for adults and children derives its effect from the quick tempo caused by fast-paced editing. Researchers who investigate these issues in television in general have noted that the response of any human to television probably has to do with the orienting response, the physiological changes that come about in the body in response to detecting movement. The pace of current television programming probably has the effect of keeping the observing human constantly attentive because of the constant stimulation of the orienting response: in fact, advertisements and music videos, as well as action sequences in televised dramas, usually change the camera angle or scene at least once per second.

This feature of television has a lot to do with its druglike effects. Over the years since its invention, the metaphor of television as drug has been more or less constantly invoked; people who watch too much television are called TV addicts, and there have been books with titles like *The Plug-in Drug*. But recently scientists have begun to document exactly how television works as an addictive activity. In a 2002 article in *Scientific American* summarizing their own and others' research in television viewing, psychologists Robert Kubey and Mihaly Csikszentmihalyi described the process roughly as follows: The television is turned on, and the pacing rivets our attention. At the same time, turning on the set also elicits a feeling of relaxation, passivity, and lowered alertness. When the set is turned off, however, people feel a continued sense of lowered alertness and passivity. Kubey and Csikszentmihalyi's research subjects report having more difficulty concentrating following television viewing, an effect that is not seen after reading or activities requiring physical exertion. Subjects in these experiments reported that they felt unfocused and somehow less positive when the television was turned off; these people reported more feelings of depression and stress after a period of television watching.

Thus, the powerful, probably not conscious pairing of a feeling of relaxation with turning on the television and the powerful association of depression and stress with turning off the television leads adult subjects to watch more television than they want to. This is not a physical addiction, in which the body calls out for more television; it is better described using a model of psychological addiction, in which there is a powerful learned but unconscious motive to turn it on (the feeling of relaxation) and a powerful learned but unconscious motive not to turn it off (the inevitable feeling of depression and stress that will follow). It is not surprising that Kubey and Csikszentmiha-lyi report data from Gallup polls in 1992 and 1999 indicating that 40 percent of adults and 70 percent of teenagers believed they spent too much time watching television.

So what? So people watch more television than they feel they should. Is there any evidence that watching television is a problem? Well, it does appear to make people stupider, if that can be described as a problem. The late introduction of television in remote communities in Canada was studied in the mid-1980s, when the introduction of cable allowed people who had no access to television finally to acquire a usable television in the home. In the homes with no television, children given a standard creativity test had higher levels of divergent thinking—that is, the ability to find many solutions to a problem—than children with a television in the home. After the introduction of television in the TV-less communities, these higher creativity scores fell to the same lower levels as those of children who had lived with television all along. Children who were now consuming other people's fantasies were clearly losing their own cognitive abilities, at least in the area of creative thinking.

❈   ❈   ❈

We come, therefore, to a conundrum. The concern voiced by most parents I know, and certainly expressed in national debates over our cultural products, is that the *content* of television is detrimental to our children's health. The calls for content censorship in the form of television ratings and V-chip technology imply that if we could only control the content of what children watch, we could rest assured that our children's health and well-being would be safeguarded. At the same time, researchers in child development and cognitive psychology have conclusively demonstrated that watching television *itself,* by its very nature, is addictive, and causes subtle but real effects on children's ability to think. But there does not seem to be any groundswell of public opinion asking our government to make television itself illegal, or to have it regulated as one would regulate other addictive substances.

Some of this may be due to the very visibility of the deleterious effects of program content. The vivid images that cause children to imitate as a way of understanding are very obvious to parents, and this effect extends beyond television to other vivid media. When children act out wrestling moves and break one another's noses in the process, or shock their parents by screaming obscenities in the manner of Eminem, the cause-and-effect relationship is obvious. It is here and now, and observable. But the effects of merely watching television—the diminished creativity, the restlessness, the intolerance of slow pacing—are less obvious to parents. These things are obvious to teachers, especially teachers who have been in the field for several years; to a person, experienced teachers assert that contemporary children as a group continue to be harder and harder to teach because they experience the slow, unvivid presentation of, say, algebra, as intolerably boring.

One could understand this conundrum as a good example of an irrational wish; parents wish that there were something that could be done to television content to make it nontoxic. At the same time (if the expressions "boob tube" or "idiot box" have any reason for living), most people know that television itself is not all that good for both children or adults. But we don't want to live without it—so we displace the worry over the medium itself onto a substitute worry, the content of what children watch.

We might even go a step further and consider whether there is some unconscious method to parental demands for content censorship. If we feel worried about the effects of television on our children, and we should be worried about it, we can feel we are doing something for them by demanding that our government, or Hollywood, or somebody do something to stop all the nasty stuff contained in the culture. And if we know—and how could we not know?—that content censorship is extremely unlikely in a society with constitutional protections on free speech and expression, we can still wish for it, knowing that it is something that may never happen.

But why don't we just turn it off? Why do parents need to ask the government, or technology, to come to the rescue? This is the interesting question now. All that bad content could be controlled with a simple flick of the switch if parents chose to do that. But most often, they do not. And the reasons are, in most cases, far from unconscious; they are simply unspoken.

OPEN SECRETS

The unspoken truths here are not unthought; these are secrets that everybody knows, and that most parents will admit to themselves and sometimes to their trusted friends or to therapists. Turning off the television would control the effects of content and the effects of the medium itself at the same time. But the open secret is that we can't live without television ourselves. We can't live without it because we want to watch it, and we can't live without it because we cannot stand not to have something that will pacify our children when we want them to be pacified or, to put it less nicely, drugged.

When parents talk about this to me, they shrug and quickly try to change the subject. They know I know what television is all about; when I'm tired, they say, I just don't want to deal with the kids, and the only thing that I can do is to plunk them down in front of the television. What more is there to say? It's embarrassing, but true. So, many parents do this without thinking about it at all. Or if they think about it, they think, Well, it's really not so bad. They use the logic of addicts, which is a peculiar logic all its own. I know cigarettes are killing me, but I'm so stressed out that I really need one right now . . . so I'll quit tomorrow. I know television is bad for them, but I'm so exhausted right now that I need to be away from them, and I need for them to be quiet, so I can relax. So they can watch television now . . . and I'll say no TV tomorrow.

Taking television addiction seriously, as an addiction, means that limiting television is intimately linked to parents' mental health. I do not mean mental health like the presence or absence of schizophrenia—I mean mental health like a reliable balance between peace and stimulation, between effort and relaxation, and between unrewarding responsibilities and rewarding engagement. But sometimes parents have already made choices that do not allow them to lead balanced lives, and when this is the case, they are in danger of becoming television addicts themselves, and their children as well, because all the preconditions necessary for this to develop are already there.

The point of any addictive substance, including television, is the speed of the perceived change in mental state. Physically, the body develops addictions, but mentally, the speed of state change is the all-powerful variable. Smoking cigarettes is really addictive because the high is instantaneous, as it is with crack and heroin. Drinking is pretty quick, but not quite as quick. Psychiatrists all know this; this is why they prescribe long-acting tranquilizers like Klonopin over short-acting tranquilizers like Ativan. Klonopin cools you out, but since you don't get the immediate kick, you are less likely to become addicted, while Ativan (which is necessary for some people with acute debilitating panic symptoms) kicks like a mule, so there is an immediate mental association between taking it and *instant* relief.

In thinking about television addiction and contemporary parenting, we can ask two fundamental questions: what did our own parents do to get instant relief from us, and why do we need so much instant relief? The first question has to do with changes in culture that seem to me relatively obvious: when our parents had too much of us, they told us to go away. If the world outside the walls of the family home was perceived as more safe then than it is now (see Chapter 1), this solution would have been much easier to apply. Parents could simply get rid of us, knowing that the neighborhood was pretty safe, and our numerous siblings and cohorts would look after us in any case. That no longer feels possible, because the world feels too dangerous—and here we can notice the interaction of television content with process. There is much published research that demonstrates that the more television people watch, the more they feel the world is a dangerous place, so the more you watch, the less you want yourself or your children to go outside anyway: they're safer inside watching TV.

The need for instant relief is a much trickier question. Almost everyone has said, on occasion, "I need a drink," and the need is usually proportional to the level of stress or exhaustion felt on the particular occasion. "I need a drink" is a way of saying, "I've had a terrible day," and the more terrible it was, the more the drink is needed. It is needed for instant relief; I need to change my mental state *right now.* This is why doctors and nurses who work in emergency rooms have a particular vulnerability to substance abuse; in addition to the availability of drugs, the nature of the work, with its unpredictable surges of stress and demands for concentration, followed by periods of quiet of unknown length, predisposes people to feel they need to relax *now,* and addictive substances are one reliable way to achieve that goal quickly.

If television researchers are right, television works in precisely the same way. It changes one's mood, it induces relaxation, *immediately.* It requires nothing of the viewer, and it is exceptionally diverting of attention, so it diverts one's attention away from the stressed-out internal world into the vacuous external world, where Buffy, a hot teenage cheerleader type, is, improbably, slaying vampires. Because it works immediately, it is going to be used in the way that all other drugs are used: to be administered when one feels stressed out. The more the stress, the more the need for immediate relief.

The use of television, therefore, is going to be intimately related to the felt pace of contemporary life. If we often feel our own lives and those of our children have been given too much gas, television is the brake. Metaphorically, we don't drive at a smooth, steady pace; we drive like maniacs, and then step on the brake when we feel out of control. As the felt pace of life approaches the felt pace of emergency room doctors and nurses, we would expect as a matter of necessity that addiction to *something* will arise. And since we can't offer our ten-year-olds a beer, we give them something else that they can use to change their mental state immediately.

It may seem paradoxical to observe that the felt fast pace of ordinary life is braked or tranquilized by fast-paced television or video entertainment. But on some level, the fast pace of stimulation does approach something like a peaceful blur. Watching old-fashioned primitive things like waterfalls or the sunset on sparkling waves, which provide a constantly shifting array of stimulation most people find peaceful, might find its analogue in a fast-paced commercial or music video or television program in which the content is unfathomable or mindless but the pace and colors are, essentially, an animated kaleido-scope.

❖　　❖　　❖

Of course, with any addictive substance, "First you take the drug, then the drug takes the drug . . ." If the model of addic-tion propounded by Kubey and Csikszentmihalyi is true, one turns on the television because of the powerful learned but un-conscious associations between TV and relaxation. Then, after it is on, the learned association between the restlessness and depression when it goes off tends to keep it on. One could cer-tainly argue that, in a family context, family coaddiction adds a powerful multiplier effect to this formula.

If I know, on some level, that I will get cranky when the television goes off, I must also know, on some level, that my kids will get cranky when the television goes off for them, even if I am not watching it. They know they will get cranky when it goes off (whether they are aware of this connection or not), and they also know I will get cranky because they will get cranky. The interaction between *(a)* my need for instant relief from the kids, which I get when they watch television, and *(b)* the instant relief I get out of television when I watch it, and *(c)* the instant relief they get when they turn it on is powerful, and all these effects happen in reverse when it goes off. So, it is more likely to stay on, even though both adults and kids report that they feel they should not watch so much TV.

*　　*　　*

The necessity for television to be calming also explains another weird phenomenon of contemporary parenting: the possession of a television by every person in the house. If parents are worried about the content of the things their children watch on television, they could get rid of all the televisions in the house. But they could also have only one television in the house, which is watched by parents and children together, so that content can be monitored the old-fashioned way: by *watching.* But this cannot be done when every kid in the house has his own television in his room: you can't go in and watch what he is watching in the middle of the night.

So why do parents buy a television for a kid's room? There is research available that demonstrates what really should not have to be demonstrated: that children's grades go down when they have their own televisions. The possibilities of watching too much, getting less sleep, and watching too much violence and sex are all raised exponentially if a child has a TV in his own room. So why would anyone do this?

Because, as every parent knows but no one likes to say out loud, it is too much trouble to negotiate what is to be watched. There are arguments over the remote. There are arguments over whose show is too boring. There are arguments at every turn, *and that ruins it as a drug experience.* Watching television goes from being pleasantly sedating to being more of the same old rat race from which you or your children are trying to escape. There is no point in sharing. Sharing a television is like drinking near beer: it doesn't get the job done. So even though every child development expert under the sun suggests that parents watch television *with* their kids, so as to monitor the content and to process their feelings and questions, there is a powerful undercurrent going in exactly the opposite direction.

What many people really want is to let their kids self-sedate in peace, which makes everyone feel more peaceful.

MEDIA CULTURE:
FINAL FACTS

The foregoing discussion should not be read as a statement that content in television, music, video games, and the Internet is not important. It is important, and there is plenty of research that demonstrates that content affects practically everything about children's thinking and behavior. In a recent summary in the *Journal of the American Academy of Child and Adolescent Psychiatry,* Dr. Susan Villani reported research evidence that heavy exposure to television, music videos, and advertising makes children more violent, more callous with respect to the feeling of others, more overstimulated, more vulnerable to consuming nicotine . . . The list goes on and on. There is considerable evidence from meta-analytic studies—those research studies which examine experimental effects from a large selection of studies on one subject—that exposure to violent content in popular culture does increase the likelihood of aggression and violence for children who consume such media, and these effects are greater the more they consume.

Indeed, the arguments in published literature mostly focus not on whether content affects behavior but on the degree to which content affects behavior. At least three related points of view have been articulated: (1) that exposure to violent media causes aggression (much like the imitative aggression discussed above) but not necessarily *violence;* (2) that exposure to violent media causes violent activity in children who are already vulnerable anyway; (3) that exposure to violent media causes actual increases in the rate of incidents of violence. In the report of the surgeon general of the United States on youth violence, released in late 2001, it was noted that there are significant findings over several decades suggesting that consumption of violent media causes aggressive behavior, but the links to actual criminal violence against persons are tenuous. These findings can be viewed in a number of ways, as evidence either that one should not be too worried about violent media or that one should be very worried, if one is taking a population-based risk management approach. Psychologists Brad Bushman and Craig Anderson summarize the latter view in their review of the impact of media violence:

> Suppose violent media make only 1% of the population more aggressive. Should society be concerned about a percentage so small? The answer should be a resounding "Yes!" Suppose 10 million people watch a violent TV program. If only 1% of the viewers will become more aggressive afterward, then the violent TV program will make 100,000 people more aggressive!

In terms of other, newer forms of media to which our children are exposed, the facts have yet to be gathered. The surgeon general's report noted the absence of published research studies on children's exposure to violent content in Internet Web sites. Research on violent video games is also relatively rare; the published studies cited in the surgeon general's report suggest that there is a small relationship between violent video games and physical aggression and a moderate relationship between violent video games and aggressive thinking. After the Columbine incident, there was an outburst of hypothesizing about the relationship between shooter video games and actual violence, but well-controlled research on these hypotheses has yet to appear in professional journals.

In thinking about these relationships in newer media, the degree of passivity must, of course, be seen as a critical factor. Both the Internet and video games require more active engagement on the part of the consumer, and of course, there is a very wide range of game styles that can be lumped under the heading of "violent content." Games that require problem solving, but not necessarily fast-paced stimulation received passively, must affect children differently than television and movies. If, as I argue here, the style of the information delivery itself—the passivity of the consumer and the accelerated pace of the product—is deleterious to children, then newer media that have less of each (to choose two obvious examples, reading an encyclopedia article on the Internet or playing a game of Myst) will be less deleterious to children.

❋   ❋   ❋

So parents who are worried about the content of our current cultural products are right to be worried, in a way. But in another way, these same parents are missing the whole point. If even *Sesame Street,* in its older, jazzier incarnation, can make children stupefied while it is on, and then restless, irritable, and bored when it goes off, why are we worrying about content control? It would be better for kids to have less violent or sexual content on television; if they are going to spend at least three hours every day watching TV, *and* we don't want to tell them not to, *and* we don't want to watch it with them, then of course we need better content control from producers or from the government. But too much of this public debate continues to be predicated on the fact that children are going to watch TV no matter what.

The most contented children I know are children who do not have television in the house at all or, if they do, have it only for use as a screen on which to watch an occasional rented movie. At a recent dinner party, a psychologist of my acquaintance was laughing about his campaign to reintroduce television into his home, in order to watch televised soccer games. His teenaged sons said, "Nope. Sorry, Dad. If we had it we'd want to watch it all the time—we're much better off without it." These kids know themselves, and the product, well enough to know that they would be tempted if it were around, so it's just better not to have it around at all. And for parents who worry about how to say no, how to say, "Turn it off," how to say, "Not tonight," and then hate themselves when they give in, it is by far the best solution.

Try This at Home

1. If you have babies or very young children, don't even let them get started with television. Let them find and develop other ways to quiet themselves down. If you read wonderfully engaging books to them early on (consult a children's librarian about this one), they will learn to love to read, because reading will always remind them of warm and close parental attention. Then they will always be able to quiet down with a book.

2. Make a list, a complete list, of everything you would really miss seeing if you got rid of your television. Make another complete list, of everything available on every channel that is trash, or worse.

3. Think about the gas-brake rhythm in your own life. If you work too hard, or your kids work too hard, and you have too little time to relax (and therefore you need to relax immediately), then you may be leading an awful life. Consider that active, engaged hobbies are possible only if you are not totally exhausted and fried from the pace of work or parenting life.

4. Place a picture of a nice cold beer on top of the television set. Then imagine that, when your child turns on the TV, he is drinking a nice cold beer instead. Do you really want him to do that?

5. Try television 1950s-style. If there is a particular show you want to watch, go to a friend's house *en famille*. Get dressed up. Bring a party platter. Watch the show all together, kind of like a Super Bowl party. You can rotate the television among the families so that the same people don't always have to clean the house. Make television watching a community, not a solitary, event.

6. Appoint a family secretary (an eight-year-old is perfect;

borrow one if you need to) and give that person a stopwatch. Ask him or her to record how much time the family spends arguing about how much TV is allowed, or what to watch, or when to turn it off. Add up all the time in a week, multiply by fifty-two, and then by eighteen (for the eighteen years the child lives at home). Doesn't it seem like an awful lot of time?

7. Send your children to a summer camp where there is no television, no Internet, no video games (including handheld devices). These camps do exist. Think of this experience as a kind of detox unit, but you don't have to be around to watch. Remove all the TVs in the house while the kids are gone.

8. When they're too noisy or overwhelming, send the kids outside. If they're not safe outside, go outside with them. Bring a book to read while you watch them out of the corner of your eye. But don't let them come in until supper.

Eight

WHEN COLUMBINE
WAS ONLY A FLOWER

A story from the year 1 P.C. (that's "Post Columbine," which was a social earthquake much bigger than political correctness, and one truly deserving of its own era):

The consulting psychologist gets a call from a distraught mother. Her sixth-grade son has been hauled in to see the principal, the guidance counselor at school, and the community police officer assigned to the school, and he has been threatened with suspension, possible expulsion, and possible legal charges.

"What did he do?" asks the worried psychologist, who knows the boy as an awkward, lonely, immature kid with a lot of good ideas and very few social skills.

"He threatened to kill everyone at school."

"What exactly did he say?" says the psychologist, thinking, Uh-oh . . . did I miss something?

"He said, and I quote, 'Those kids at Columbine had the right idea.' "

The veracity of the quote is not in question. The other kids heard it, the kid admitted having said it, and the possible punishments being considered all follow from a true accounting of the facts. But the facts from the kid's point of view are a little more complicated. His account goes something like this: He was in his science lab and he was, as usual, being teased by the other kids. He is known to get mad easily, and when teased, to get red in the face and say something stupid, which is greatly amusing to the other kids in his class. So, in his science lab, he was getting picked on again, and he wanted the teasing to stop, and the other kids wouldn't stop. He told me later, "I wanted to think of something that would make them stop. I thought if I really scared them they might go away. So I said, 'Those kids at Columbine had the right idea.' And you know what? They all looked scared and then went away and left me alone."

If the consulting therapist said "uh-oh" before, there is a lot more reason to say it now. We now have a child who feels powerless, who has difficulty in social skills and has a history of social isolation, and we have given him a big fat secret weapon. It is not a real weapon, a gun or a bomb; it is a word, and the word is "Columbine." When he utters the magic word, scary tormenting kids scatter like little mice. In the power of the moment, he forgets that uttering this word, which will bring short-term gains—everyone will feel terrified and leave him alone—will also bring long-term losses: the adults in the community will take actions to label him as a scary deviant of whom everyone should feel afraid.

Now, I am well aware that threatening people is a crime. The crime is a form of assault, and making people feel terrified is an action punishable by the law, for grown-ups as well as kids. It is not okay to go around saying, "I'm going to kill you," and most school personnel who are trying to make schools safe are trying very hard to make sure that everyone feels safe. That means cracking down on every form of violence, even threatened violence. But there's the proverbial rub: in a climate of fear, when everyone feels unsafe, and the "crime" is making someone feel unsafe, how do we know when a crime has been committed?

In the aftermath of the Columbine school shootings in 1999, the wave of fear that passed over the parent population in this country was unprecedented in its scope and reach. Parents I knew were terrified about whether their children were safe at school, and this fear led to one big response: try to find out who the next perpetrator is, and stop him before he kills everybody in school. Kids who were loners, or kids with bad tempers, or kids who were confusing or awkward, or wore funny clothes, were, all over the country, subjected to a new kind of scrutiny, which to many of the kids involved seemed like a kind of double jeopardy.

Indeed, the logic of the immediate post-Columbine era defied logic. It went something like this: The Columbine shooters were kids who had been picked on and mocked by other kids. They got angry and decided to seek revenge, and did, in a horrible way. Therefore, kids who are picked on and mocked and who might be angry about it are the likeliest to be perpetrators of school violence. The kids who need to be rounded up, identified, and targeted for intervention, then, are the kids who are mocked by, or subjected to violence from, other kids.

And in the days immediately after the shootings, unusual or divergent kids all over the country were targeted as potential criminals. Social psychologist Elliot Aronson reported many such anecdotes in his book *Nobody Left to Hate: Teaching Compassion After Columbine*. One example: "A few days after the Columbine tragedy, my sixteen-year-old grandson came home from school and said, 'Guess what? The principal sent around a notice asking us to report any kids who are dressing strangely, behaving weirdly, appear to be loners, or out of it.'"

What was obvious to even the most casual observer at the time was that the well-intentioned efforts to prevent another Columbine were having the effect of taking isolated people and isolating them further. If the embrace of the school community is what outcast kids are lacking, it probably doesn't help to take actions that label them as dangerous potential killers. Nobody liked them already, but now that the adults in the school have essentially told everybody they are lethal, they are not likely to get more invitations to prom parties—it's just not going to happen. It seemed pretty clear that this approach, trying to identify potential school shooters and isolate them from the school community, had great potential for making the problem worse.

Now, here's where the issue gets really tough. As we noted in Chapter 5, the process of socialization always involves a balance between a child's right to be special and a community's right to have a child be not special—to be governed by rules just like everybody else. And the rules and priorities of school administrators are, and need to be, squarely on the side of the rights of the community: the right of the people in the community to feel safe, the right of the community to be orderly, the right of children and parents to go to school without fear. But as in any other situation of domestic emergency, the rights of suspicious-looking people get trampled. This is inevitable; people who are charged with ensuring public safety sometimes have to err on the side of caution.

The issue here does, however, go beyond fairness or empathy for the outcast individual. It goes beyond the inevitable clampdown in a response to an emergency (or in the case of Columbine, a felt emergency: the real risks of such an attack are actually pretty low, as we shall see). The issue is whether the immediate response of identifying potential perpetrators actually makes things worse. One could argue that what is needed as a response to a Columbine-type event is further community building, not further community splintering.

Let's look back at an earlier example. In Chapter 1, I told a true story of a parent who felt anxious about school violence. She had heard about her child's classmate's reputation for violence: the child had hit someone in the class in the previous year and the mother thought the child "looked mean." She asked the consulting therapist whether she should home-school her second-grade daughter, so that she would know she was safe. The mother's impulse is a completely natural one: that kid might be dangerous—and I want to keep my child away from him. It is a response any parent would have, and it is completely normal.

From the point of view of the "dangerous" child, however, *and* from the practical point of view of preventing further trouble down the road, this kind of isolation makes things worse. Many divergent children do start being isolated very early, because they look funny, or their eye contact is a little off, or they don't quite know what to say. Such isolation is already something that children do to one another, but it is magnified a hundredfold when the adults in the picture help the process along by helping to isolate the divergent child. By the time the child gets to be in, say, fifth or sixth grade, he already has years of people shunning him to feel angry about. The process of social isolation makes the child less socialized, more disconnected from the community, and more likely, I would argue, to act in an antisocial way.

Children of a certain age punish nonconformity pretty ruthlessly. Kids who are picked on or teased or ignored by their classmates are a heterogeneous group: they are kids who may develop mental illness, or already be mentally ill; kids who may be potentially violent, or already be violent; kids whose parents have funny foreign accents; kids who are too tall or too short, or too early in puberty or too late in puberty—the list goes on and on. Kids are adept at finding out who is really abnormal, but it is because they cast a pretty wide net. They make what statisticians call a Type I error: they find all the true positives, but they identify a lot of false positives along the way.

We can assume, therefore, that kids who are truly headed for a life of violence, whether because of organic impulse-control difficulties, mental illness, histories of abuse, or some combination thereof, will be identified early and shunned by other kids. We can also assume that kids will make a lot of mistakes, and they will shun or isolate a lot of kids who are marginal: odd, or quirky, or temperamental, but not really violent and not headed toward a life of violence. But this kind of shunning, or isolation, will make the marginal kids more marginal, more angry, more furious, and more (at least in fantasy) interested in fantasies of revenge. It is not because of readers' identification with the sadistic, tormenting popular crowd of high schoolers that Stephen King's first novel, *Carrie*, was such an enormous hit; it was because of readers' identification with Carrie herself, the kid who was picked on a little too much and discovered she had the power to get even in a big way. Most of these readers were not violent people—just people who had been outcasts, or had felt like outcasts, somewhere along the way. And for every kid who felt like an outcast when he was a kid, there is a kid who participated in excluding him and now has no idea why.

Most kids are afraid, for their own developmental reasons, of kids who are different; we know that, and we can forgive them for it, because they are kids. But it is the job of adults to correct the Type I errors that kids make—if kids paint every unusual kid with a broad brush, the least we can expect of ourselves is to refine the portraits they are painting. In the atmosphere of panic that followed the Columbine shootings, many parents gave up and decided that the safest thing to do is to go with the Type I error themselves: any kid who was unusual was a suspect. And making a kid a suspect might be useful for identifying the kids who truly have the potential to be violent, but making suspects of all the kids who are marginal has the effect of isolating isolated children further from a real community. *In this case, hitting the panic button just makes things worse.*

The psychology of the Type I error is deeply embedded in the psychology of worrying. Indeed, the Type I error—that is, being willing to identify and deal with kids who are false positives in the search for potential troublemakers—is psychologically identical to the errors made by any obsessive-compulsive person. If a person is phobic about germs and feels, rightly, that contact with a stray germ for a deadly disease can cause a fatal illness, that person can turn his life upside down committing the Type I error: he can wash his hands endlessly, wear masks every time he goes out in public, avoid the public entirely, and spend all day washing floors and household surfaces. The person engaged in such activity is probably reducing his exposure to germs, but may be greatly reducing the quality of his life in the process. Most people are content to take reasonable precautions and, in situations where the probability of infection by a stray germ is quite small, are willing to take the chance in order to preserve a quality of life that feels reasonably sane. One could also argue that efforts to keep the body reasonably healthy will mean that the germ, if encountered, won't kill you anyway, even if it makes you sick.

Since school violence is an extremely rare event, chasing the phenomenon around may be a lot like chasing germs around. The stakes are extraordinarily high if one believes that murder is a likely outcome of school violence (which it is not; see below). For parents who have decided that they will never, ever allow their children to be exposed to a risk, however small, chasing potentially violent kids around is like chasing germs; it consumes an alarming amount of time and resources with very little, if any, return on the investment.

Psychologists who study the prediction of violence have been trying, with little apparent success, to swim against the tide of public opinion by pointing out that reducing the problem of school violence to one of identifying, and expelling, potential perpetrators is a solution that is far too simple to be effective because the phenomenon of school violence is extraordinarily complicated. If school violence is an outcome with many predictors, the predictive factors are extremely numerous. Children are still developing, and therefore, developmental factors such as physical development, including brain development, may intervene and affect an outcome in a *potentially* violent youth. The development of impulse control in the maturing brain can help a potentially violent child control himself, just as a brain injury or exposure to a disinhibiting substance can help a seemingly nonviolent child lose control. One ritual in the aftermath of a spectacular episode of violence, whether the perpetrator was a child or an adult, is the news report in which neighbors and friends or family members look into the television camera and swear that this person is someone from whom one would least expect an act of violence. Thinking ungenerously, we could see this as just more evidence of human stupidity; we all reassure ourselves that, if *we* had been the neighbors or friends of that terrible criminal, *we* would have read all the signs correctly. It is this little assertion of human omnipotence that allows us to get out of bed every morning without too much fear. But a more charitable, and true, reading of the ritual disavowals by the neighbors and friends is that, in fact, human violence is awfully hard to predict, and things happen by chance that sometimes tip people over from one course of action into another.

Experts who study youth violence also point out that the social matrix for the development of violence is exceedingly complex, and makes the simple model of isolating the potential perpetrator a hopeless task. Psychologists Edward Mulvey and Elizabeth Cauffman, in a recent review of these issues, noted that youth violence is not usually the province of loners: 60 percent of youths who committed assaults and 90 percent of youths who committed robberies were with peers at the time of the offense. Mulvey and Cauffman also point out that complicated social events can interact to turn potential violence into lethal action, and these events can include taunting or teasing by peers, rejection by boyfriends or girlfriends, and rejection or lack of interest from parents. Children who turn to lethal action are children who feel that they have nothing to lose, which means that whatever they had in the form of love relationships and supportive family members has already been experienced as lost. The potential for calamity in the lives of vulnerable children is always present, and it is certainly beyond the scope of the adult community to control.

One does not have to worry about all the complications in

the lives of potentially violent children if the simple goal is to treat them like germs, that is, to get rid of them. And since kids are a lot more complicated than germs, they can frequently help to get rid of other kids. The cycle of identification and isolation of potential troublemakers, which is infinitely worse since the Columbine killings, frequently does result in children who are potentially violent leaving the school community, but the community as a whole is not served by this activity.

Let's return to our threatening sixth-grader, the one who uses the C-word—"Columbine"—to drive kids away. When he does this, he drives kids away temporarily. He also gets to visit the community police officer and the school principal, who remind him that threatening people, making them feel unsafe, is a crime. If he continues, he may be suspended, or prosecuted, because he can't be allowed to stay in school if he commits a crime. He is, by definition, a kid who blows up easily, and the grown-ups have now added this little extra straw to his already heavy burden; if he gets teased and blows up (which is one reason he gets teased in the first place), he might also be isolated further. He does not want to be isolated. In fact, he wants to be accepted. But the extra anxiety about the consequences of losing control somehow makes keeping in control a little bit harder. Two months later, when he blows up again (this time remembering not to use the C-word), he is reminded by all the adults that he is on thin ice, and further incidents of making children feel unsafe will not be tolerated.

Meanwhile, the other kids pick on him more. They do not do this to be malicious, but they do this because they are worried, too. They know the kid is explosive, and now they know, by observing the actions of the adults around him, that he is also dangerous. It might make sense to leave him alone, but picking on him is like picking a scab: it is uncomfortable not knowing if or when he is going to blow, and one can have some control over that by making it happen. So he gets picked on more and more. And he blows up again and again.

This kid is not going to make it. Sooner or later, he will

blow up once too often, and he will be asked to leave, or expelled, or suspended so many times that he is essentially exiled anyway. From the outside, one can see how the adults in authority, and the other kids, and the child himself all collude to get him put outside the community. And when he does leave (and by the way, this is a real child we're talking about, and he really did leave his school community after several such events), the school personnel can feel a little guilty and also very relieved, because *we don't have to worry anymore about whether or not he will hurt our kids.* The fact that he still lives down the street, and he is now really angry about having been pushed out, does not seem to enter into the safety equation. Some school and workplace shooters, in fact, are people who come back to the place that has expelled them to exact retribution.

One way to stop this train wreck might have been for the school personnel to try to absorb some of the anxiety. The school administrators might have said, through their actions, "I know this kid makes everybody nervous; but he's probably not really violent, and we're going to try to make him and everyone else feel safe by working extra hard to include him in our community." This might have worked. But in an era of extreme worrying about school violence, it takes an extraordinarily courageous school administration to protect the community by enlarging it and making it more tolerant and inclusive. And one reason this courage is required is the worries of the school administrators' ultimate bosses, the parents, who are deeply embroiled in the psychology of scapegoating.

THE SCAPEGOAT FANTASY

Scapegoating is both a fantasy and a reality, and most people know something about both sides of this ancient phenomenon. The fantasy side is the more powerful, and it speaks to us about the ultimate fate of the struggle between the individual and the community. Since I am not a theologian, I cannot speak with authority here about the big issues involved in this myth, including the issues of martyrdom and purification of a community by one member being chosen to take upon himself the job of purification through self-sacrifice.

I am referring to the dark side of scapegoating, the process by which an anxious community decides it must save itself by sacrificing one of its members. When a community is having a bad time, one time-honored and too-simple solution is to seek out the one member of the community whose evil deeds have brought the bad times for all. When that community member can be identified, he or she can be sacrificed, and the community can feel safe again because the source of the anxiety has been eradicated. This is a powerful wish, and one that infects every human community to a greater or lesser degree. It is also a self-perpetuating myth, and it is very hard to disprove; if a scapegoat is sacrificed, and the community is still anxious or miserable, the problem is not with scapegoating itself, but just the selection of the wrong scapegoat.

The reality of this myth is that everyone knows how it operates, and everyone expects, with some degree of grim certitude, that it must operate. When something bad happens, we say someone has to take the fall. Implicit in this remark is the knowledge that bad behavior in a community is frequently widely distributed, but for the community to be seen, and to see itself, as just and right, someone needs to be punished *as if* they were the one responsible party and *as if* the banishment of the scapegoat will purify the community. Even if some people, deep down, know that the much-desired community purification is unlikely to be achieved by the sacrifice of a single scapegoat, almost everyone believes, when a community is in crisis, that such a sacrifice will be demanded and this demand must be respected.

In school communities that are in crisis—a school community being broadly defined as the children and their parents, the teachers and administrators—the need to find a scapegoat is just as powerful as in every other community. The real feeling

"We need to do something" is often subtly, or not so subtly, translated into "We need to find out who is responsible for making us feel worried and get rid of them so we don't feel worried anymore." If the worrying is really bad, as it was in every school community following the relentless press coverage of the Columbine killings, the need for a scapegoat can escalate even if there is a countervailing wish to preserve the integrity of the community.

This is most easily observed on the level of the child's classroom, even in elementary schools, where, presumably, lethal violence is not the issue. In some classroom communities, a child who is an outlier can sometimes be identified as *the* source of anxiety. As a consultant, I sometimes hear this as, "Everything would be all right in my child's class if it weren't for [insert scapegoat's name here]," or sometimes, "She would be having a great time at school if it weren't for [scapegoat]." And it is true, or true enough, that outlier children, the ones who are at the far end of the bell-shaped curve for activity level, or aggression, or impulsivity, make everyone's life a little more challenging. The logic of scapegoating, which many parents imply and many openly embrace, is that the child in question needs to be thrown out or expelled. Sometimes this is expressed in a less radical form—the child doesn't have to leave the community, but "I want you to keep that kid away from my kid at all times and in all respects"—a wish for a kind of internal restraining order that is not so easy to enforce in a class with twenty-two children and one adult.

The logic of scapegoating is ultimately unworkable, because the feeling of peace and relief that an anxious community feels after an expulsion is only temporary (that is why the good townspeople in Shirley Jackson's story have a lottery every year). The other logical problem with scapegoating is that outliers are a statistical reality that will not go away until everyone in the community is identical. There is always a "worst kid in the class," by definition. I have been known, when I am having a less than kind day, to express this knowledge in the following statement to an angry parent: "I know it seems as if the class would be better if the school got rid of [scapegoat]. But then, after that, there will be another kid in the class who seems like the worst troublemaker in the room. How do you know that next kid won't be yours?" This is mean, in a way, but it does sometimes have the salutary effect of reminding someone that a community is made up of individuals, and once the community gets rolling on sacrificing individuals, it might be hard to stop when it gets to your child.

Parents have a right to expect that their children will be physically protected at school. Schools need to have rules that work, and rules that work need to have an ultimate bottom line, which is expulsion. This is a reality that is not going to go away, and parents should not have to put up with their children being the victims of violence. But a threat, or a feeling of unsafety, is a big gray area, and parents who require of their children's school that their children, and they themselves, will never, ever feel even a little eensy bit threatened by another child may be asking too much of their school.

Inclusion requires great reserves of equanimity, something we don't all have all the time, but here's what school administrators can say to a parent when there is a demand to get rid of a scary kid: "I know you're scared, but what we know from research on this problem is the thing that best prevents school violence is for each child to feel that school is fair, and for each child to feel a connection to the other kids and the adults in his school. [Scapegoat] isn't feeling too connected to our school community at present. I'm trying to help him with that. Can you think of a way to help, too?" It also requires reserves of equanimity for a parent to say, "I feel a little scared about [scapegoat]. Is there something I can do to help out with him or his family so that he doesn't feel even more isolated from the community?" Parents are not saints, any more than anyone else, but it is not only good but also practical to help build school communities, because strengthening the school community is one big thing that actually works to prevent school violence.

GROWN-UPS AND CLIQUES

One of the most fascinating elements of discussions of the Columbine tragedy is the discussion of cliques in high school. Every school has them: jocks, preps, freaks, the drama club, the band geeks, as well as the more colorful local variants like those described by Elliot Aronson in his hometown of Santa Cruz: "in descending order of importance, there are the jocks, the preppies, the surfers, the roamers, the nerds, the goths and the dirts." We all know about this, having been there when we were kids.

But what is not said in these discussions is that we are all still there. The late Meg Greenfield, star political reporter for the *Washington Post* and *Newsweek,* understood this, and in a book she was working on at the time of her death, she described the world of Washington, D.C., as one big high school, with familiar cliques operating in ways more or less like those we all remember. Certainly our current president is familiar to most of us as a high school jock/preppie type, although the last one was just as certainly an anomalous hybrid.

People whose personalities or abilities push them into particular social niches in high school seem to stay in them. People who were football stars in high school go on to be professional football players, if they were very good, or high school football coaches, if they were less good. It is extremely rare to find a high school football coach who did not play football in high school, just as it is extremely rare to find a professional musician or music teacher who did not play an instrument in high school. We don't shed those identities when we graduate, and we don't shed the prejudices, either. The social skills, good looks, and ambition that make for success in high school also make for success after high school, and people often gravitate to the same niches they always had. The crossover person—the high school computer nerd who ends up in elective office, or the popular beauty queen who ends up as a mortician—is the exception, not the rule.

What grown-ups leave out of the discussion when talking about cliques in high school is that they retain their old prejudices. The insider/outsider identities that we formed then don't magically go away, and they continue to inform our projections of our values onto our children. Elliot Aronson makes the touching point in his book that the killers at Columbine were acting as a result of the extreme pressure of being mocked and tormented by "insiders" in their high school, and he notes with some dismay that model interventions, based upon sound social psychological research, have been available *for decades* that might alleviate insider/outsider conflicts in high schools. But he fails to address why, if such interventions have been available all this time, so few schools use them.

In my work with children and parents, I am no longer surprised by this particular disjunction between concern and action. Because I work in a small community, I have often had the experience of hearing parents of some children talk about other children whom I also happen to know as my patients. It is no longer surprising to me to hear, in one hour, a terribly sad teenager talk about how his classmates torment him, and later in the day, to hear a scathing comment from another parent about the scary weirdo in his child's class—and they happen to be the same kid.

There is a truth of human nature at work here that is not going to go away anytime soon. Children who are popular in elementary and middle school, and to a slightly lesser degree, teenagers who are popular in high school, are kids who appear to be "normal." Popularity itself, which as every school kid knows, is different from likability, is a projection onto certain kids of everyone's wish to be normal. In an evolutionary sense, psychological normality is like physical beauty: people are attracted to physically beautiful people because (if evolutionary psychologists are right, and I think in this case they are) beauty means something on a very deep, animal level. Beauty means reproductive fitness; symmetry, robustness, broad shoulders in men and full lips in women mean, to our animal selves, that mating with this person would produce healthy, fit offspring. Psychological normality may mean the same thing: people who seem to be free of kinks may have a deep appeal to a primitive part of ourselves that hungers for a mate with the psychological equivalent of reproductive fitness. Divergence, or difference from some normal ideal, may be, on some biological level, deeply unappealing to our children and to ourselves. This may explain, to social scientists like Aronson, why many adults find it hard to do the work of making a school culture that embraces differences; there may be a part of all of us that believes that the work should be done by the outsider weirdos, who should be working harder to fit in, instead of the work being done by the insider normals, to try to make weirdness welcome.

The worries that we have about school violence can be driven by these age-old, not conscious issues. We are all still wearing our not-quite-outgrown high school or junior high school uniforms in our heads, and these old identifications can make us worry in some pretty distorted ways. On the one hand, there is the deep distrust we have of outsiders and their unpredictability, their nonnormalcy, as well as the aggression we might imagine from them, which comes as retaliation for the aggression visited upon them by . . . us, if we feel like insiders. The deep paranoia can work the other way, of course, with those who still feel like outsiders expecting persecution from a normal majority. Either way, the old tribal ways die hard, and when we see our children moving into or around the same tribes, our own worries can certainly get stirred up.

NARCS AND WHISTLEBLOWERS

The other, not unconscious but often unspoken truth that gets in the way of combating school violence is the adult world's hatred of snitches. Actually, "snitch" is a lovely old-fashioned word that few people use anymore, but the concept is still as sound as ever. Whether we think of them as tattletales or narcs, many adults have a real aversion to children who report other children's wrongdoing to adults. We often tell children not to be tattletales, and we often express, to our children, our overt or unspoken distaste for children who wish to ingratiate themselves with adults by reporting the bad deeds of others.

Okay. When we were children, we hated snitches and tattletales and narcs for a good reason. When we were kids trying to get away with something, there was nothing worse than a kid who would blow our plans by telling the grown-ups. But guess what? We're not kids anymore. We're the grown-ups, and not snitching is a value held by teenagers and career criminals that we might want to rethink as a value we hold and covertly reinforce by our obvious distaste for tattletales.

In schools, this is changing rapidly in the post-Columbine era. School administrators tell me, emphatically, that the thing they need to depend on now is for kids to come forward when they know something scary is happening. At a school in my neck of the woods, there was recently a celebration of community heroism for children who snitched: when they found out that a child had brought a gun to school, they told their teacher. Sure enough, he had brought a gun to school, and although it wasn't loaded, there were also some bullets for it that happened to be floating around the building. The children who told what they knew were publicly thanked and rewarded by the adults, and given the equivalent of medals of honor for this behavior; and in my view, this was a wonderful action on the part of the adult community.

In the world of adults, we call this whistleblowing, and we typically see it as a good thing. People who are involved in a lawbreaking operation and who try to tell the world, like Sherron Watkins of Enron fame, are justly rewarded by the approbation of the community for trying to stop crime. We do all we can to try to make sure that whistleblowers are not punished by their fellows, who might be tempted to do them in for blowing the whistle.

As a community of adults we can also get behind this by upholding these values for our children. When one is an adult whose job it is to uphold authority and to curb the excesses of youth, whistleblowers are valuable assets. Kids who do this protect themselves and one another. But if we, as adults, still think of ourselves as kids, and still wish to uphold the values of kids, we might not be too comfortable with whistleblowers. The effects of pathological integrity can be seen here as well: if we ask of ourselves that our values not change from youth into adulthood, or if we think it would be hypocritical to vilify narcs in our youth and then praise them when we are adults, we are falling into the same old trap. We are putting our own integrity, or continuity, or ennobled sense of our (adolescent) self, ahead of our children's welfare. Adults' expressed distaste for tattletales is a powerful message; so why do we want to send it?

In this case, parents' worries about their children's safety is probably increased by the partially conscious, but sometimes disowned, knowledge that we have trained them not to tattle. So when it becomes a matter of life and death that they *do* tattle, those of us who taught them not to tattle might be a little more anxious than we would like to be. If we have taught them that childhood is a secret society, we might get a little more nervous when they have really important secrets that they're not telling.

SCHOOL VIOLENCE:
THE FACTS

The worst-case worry for any parent thinking about school violence is the worry that one's child will be killed at school. Mulvey and Cauffman point out, in their review, that figures on adolescent death demonstrate the extreme unlikeliness of this kind of tragedy: less than 1 percent of homicides and suicides among adolescents occur in or around school grounds. The National Youth Violence Prevention Resource Center reported that in the academic year 1998–99, the year that nineteen teenagers were killed at Columbine High School, there were fifty school-related violent deaths in the United States, of which thirty-four were homicides of children and youth; this represented a drop from a high of forty-nine homicides during the academic year 1995–96. Most homicides of youth occur in inner cities and in neighborhoods outside of school, according to the Center for the Study and Prevention of Violence at Colorado State University. The center notes that from the years 1992 to 1999, a total of 190 people were slain in shooting incidents in American schools, including faculty and students. At the same time, the center estimated, between six and seven children and youth were slain in the United States every day, mostly in poor and inner-city neighborhoods.

Clearly children and teenagers being killed is a big problem in the United States, but it is not in schools that the problem exists. Children in neighborhoods with a great deal of poverty and social disorganization are at the greatest risk, as they always have been. As I noted in the Introduction, those are the kids who need worrying about. But for them, as for all kids, school is just about the safest place to be.

Try This at Home

1. Imagine a school in which everyone's talents were equally celebrated. Imagine if each and every school activity, from the band to the debate team to the local chapter of Future Farmers of America, had its own energetic, attractive, popular cheerleaders. Instead of thinking about why this wouldn't work, try to make it work.
2. Reread Shirley Jackson's "The Lottery."
3. If you have a very young child, take the time to invite, for a play date in your home, a schoolmate nobody likes. When your child gets a little older, she won't ask this child over voluntarily, so do it now when you're still calling the shots. If everyone does this, maybe that child

will not be totally alienated and furious by the time she is a teenager.

4. Take some time—it won't take long—to remember your tribe in high school. Take the time to observe whether your child's tribe is the same as yours was, or different. If your child's tribe is of a higher status than yours was, can you live with it? Is it possible that you expect retribution from your former tribe—that they will come and claim your child, and you, because you're not really jocks or preps, you're really hippies, or goths, or maybe even dirts, who are just trying to pass?

5. If your tribe was pretty low, and your child's is too, and he or she is getting picked on, can you try to be rational about this?

6. Try to remember that normality, like beauty, is bestowed by chance or divine providence, but not by ourselves. Homely kids can do what they can, but they will never be beautiful; unusual kids can do what they can, but they cannot will themselves to be normal. Sometimes they can will themselves to *act* normal, and sometimes this is a prudent course of action. Try to remind your kid that, by the end of high school, none of this will matter.

Nine

BUT WHAT
ABOUT THEM?

This book ends with the question that many parents might have wanted answered right up front. We have seen that parental worrying is a problem for parents; too many life decisions are made on the basis of worry-driven and unhelpful information. And we have seen that much of our worrying as parents is displaced—it is real enough, but it is our own worrying about ourselves, which we have projected onto our children so that we don't have to feel so bad about whatever it is that is really bothering us. We can worry about their competitive lives, or their corruption by the media, or their safety in school, and therefore not have to think about our own worries. But if parents can become aware of the facts and the fantasies that drive parental worrying, maybe we can all lead better, less worried lives.

At the outset of this book, I stated that I do not believe that parental worrying is a crisis *for children*. If worrying is extra, useless mental energy by definition, then it probably has very little effect on children. As I discussed in Chapter 3, vigilance does have an effect; listening for a toddler who might at any moment go crashing down the stairs might just have the effect of preserving the life of that toddler. But worrying, the thing that continues when useful vigilance is at an end, must have a limited effect. Worrying about a plane crash when you are on the plane doesn't hold the plane up in the air, but it doesn't make it crash, either. It just has no effect. In the same way, we might suppose that parental worrying has little effect on children as well.

In this chapter, I would like to speculate about the effects of parental worrying on our children and on our society. As I have noted, the research that would prove or disprove such guesswork has not yet been done; the necessary research would measure parental worrying across generations, and look at relevant features of children's lives that might be affected by excesses of parental worrying. Since the intuition that we worry too much is relatively recent, we don't have this research available. As the researchers from the public advocacy group Public Agenda noted, we just haven't asked questions like "Is it harder to be a parent now than it was for your own parents?" of anyone but current parents. Since tracking the amount of parental worrying is in its infancy, we can be forgiven for not being able to know what such worrying does to our children or our society.

In many ways, the following hypotheses are not about parental worrying itself as a force affecting societal change. The major causative factors may be the factors that cause parental worrying in the first place: small family sizes, a (mis)perception of the world as a more dangerous place than ever, and the effects of parents from large generations of children projecting their own generational experience onto their own small families, to name a few. In this sense, parental worrying is a link in a chain, and not the first link.

One of the places to look at the effect of parental worrying is in the area of integrity, both of parents and of children. Many have argued that integrity, or honor, or trustworthiness, in American society is on a long, not-so-slow decline, and many who believe this also point to the increased competitiveness of American society as a culprit. Whether this is true, or could be proven to be true, is beyond the scope of this book. But perceived competitiveness—the feeling that "the world is so much more competitive today"—may be contributing to a decline in the integrity of parents as a group; because worries about children's futures loom so large, everything else, even simple honesty, starts to shrink by comparison.

Take the example of plagiarism. Plagiarism scandals are endemic of late, thanks to the easy availability of essays, term papers, and reports that students can purchase or simply pirate over the Internet. Plagiarism is a crime that many schools take very seriously, and work pretty hard to eradicate. A typical student handbook or code of honor, in many American high schools, lays out penalties for plagiarism, and these penalties are usually severe: at least a grade of zero for the plagiarized work, and sometimes suspension or other, more serious penalties.

But parents don't always agree with the student handbook. In a case that made the national headlines in 2002, a teacher in Piper, Kansas, resigned after she discovered that many of her students in high school biology had plagiarized term papers off the Internet. She gave them stiff penalties, as she thought she was supposed to do, and found herself being reprimanded by the local school board and being forced to change the failing grades she gave to her students. The teacher's resignation, as a matter of principle, was hailed nationwide as an example of one courageous individual taking a stand against moral decline. But what about that moral decline?

We can assume a few things about this outbreak of moral

degeneracy. Maybe the good people of Piper, Kansas, are not good people, and there is something in the air or the water that is making them corrupt. Maybe the town was settled by gangsters, and these children are just following in their parents' footsteps. Or maybe the good people of Piper, Kansas, are so worried about their children's future that, when their children get into serious trouble, they get scared and try to make everything turn out okay.

It is easy to rain down moral condemnation from afar. It is also easy to imagine that if this were your kid, and they were getting a zero on a big biology project, which would lower their term grade from a nice 90 or 91 to a 60 or 61, and you were concerned about their rank in class and their prospects for getting in to a good college, you might lean on the school committee to give them a break. You might have been, or I might have been, one of those parents who say, "They've learned their lesson—don't make them pay for it *for the rest of their lives*," because, as we believe, if they don't get into a superselective college, they will pay for it for the rest of their lives.

What price do we put on integrity? At what point do we say, "Yes, my kid screwed up and it's time he learned his lesson"? Parents who are perfectly willing to ground their children, and give them consequences at home, and uphold the law in every way, suddenly get weak knees when they believe that a consequence for a child's bad behavior will be a part of his permanent record. I do believe that, as a consequence of worries about our children in a competitive world, we think less than we should about the part of the permanent record that really is permanent: a child's observation of our own integrity.

There is another example, a little closer to home, that can be pointed to with some confidence in terms of a real, observable trend in this department. That phenomenon is the question of untimed SATs. As we know, SAT tests do figure prominently in a teenager's college application portfolio and, although they may be losing some of their prestige and magical status, they are still, in the minds of many parents, pretty important. Parents spend fortunes on SAT prep courses for their children, and children spend a huge amount of time in these courses trying to buff their shiny exteriors to a very high gloss.

But SAT tests are timed, and that is part of the reason they are difficult. They would be a lot easier if they were untimed, and at some point in the last ten years a lot of parents figured that out. (The *Boston Globe* reported in 1997 that requests for untimed SATs because of learning disabilities doubled from a total of eight thousand in 1991 to sixteen thousand in 1996.) Parents figured out that children with documented learning disabilities can take untimed SATs, and starting in the year 2003, the asterisk that used to denote "nonstandard testing conditions" will be removed from all reports of SAT scores. It didn't take long for many parents to try to get some kind of learning disability documented for their children, even children who had never had any special education services and children whose parents would not have dreamed of having them labeled, when they were younger, as "special ed kids." According to a front-page story in the *New York Times* in September 2002, school psychologists are now seeing a steady uptick in requests for special education diagnoses, a phenomenon the *Times* calls "diagnosis-shopping."

Now, the area of learning disability is a legal nightmare anyway, as any child advocate knows. Not all children learn in exactly the same way, and the cutoff between learning *differences* that fall in the range of normal variation and true learning *disabilities* is a line so fine as to be sometimes invisible. One cannot fault parents for fearing that their children's learning differences might put them at a disadvantage in taking timed tests. But the recent spike in the request for untimed tests, and the aggressiveness with which many parents have pursued this option, suggested something else was going on—something that might be described as bending the rules, or maybe even little white lies.

When parents are frankly cooking up a disability, children know it. They know when they all of a sudden have an advantage that they never had before; and they know, when their parents ask them not to talk about it, that they are participating in a little con job. This little con job might be seen as continuous with all the other little con jobs that go into the college application process, like inflating those little volunteer hours to make them look like real self-sacrifice, or reporting the honorable mentions that everyone in that particular activity got just for participating. Making yourself look good to a prospective employer is a part of life, and it's not a bad thing to learn. But when it goes over into faking disabilities in order to gain competitive advantage, it may have gone too far.

A third, more worrisome example of where integrity is going is the drinking scandal that erupted in the affluent New York City suburb of Scarsdale in September of 2002. At the annual homecoming dance, scores of students, according to national wire service reports, showed up at school in states of acute intoxication from drinking at private house parties before the dance. Five of the students were hospitalized with acute alcohol poisoning, and "scores" of students were falling-down drunk, according to the *New York Times,* which described the scene as a "bacchanal." The *Times* also reported the discouraging news that some parents called the school after the fact in an effort to reverse their children's suspensions from school, fearing the effect on—what else?—college admissions.

As we all know from reading the business section of the newspapers, life is full of slippery slopes. This particular slope has potential for real slippage, because it is so hard to talk about, let alone legislate. For parents whose only motive is "I would do anything for my kids," it is sometimes not so hard to add a little private truth torturing to the list. And it truly is a slippery slope because it starts with such a pure motive, and it is so hard to see helping your kid evade punishment as a form of corruption.

But when children see it, they do one of two things, neither of them good. First, they start to think that truth torturing is generally okay, because they don't know that their otherwise upright parents limit their truth torturing to child-forwarding activities. Second, they start to feel guilty about the truth torturing and start to sabotage themselves to make up for it. Children are moral pilgrims, and in many cases they are willing to sacrifice themselves to rectify some advantage they have received that feels, to them, unfair. So it is not surprising when children who have been the beneficiaries of little white lies start to fail anyway—many of them are just trying to restore goodness in the world by not allowing corruption to take root. In either case, the effort to give one's kid a leg up sometimes ends up making things worse for the child involved. It might also make things worse in general for society, if more people grow up thinking this kind of behavior is okay.

There may be some steps we can take to forestall this depressing state of affairs. If we stop believing that the world is so terribly competitive for our children, maybe we can stop creepy, dishonest interventions on their behalf. In this way, making ourselves less anxious can not only make us feel better, but make the world a little better at the same time.

WORRIED PARENTS, WORRIED SOCIETY

The whole phenomenon of cheating on children's behalf is part of a larger moral quandary. As in any other domain of life, we need rules to keep everyone else in check, but we might also have some kind of competitive advantage if we somehow bend the rules, or gain an advantage before anyone else does. Joan Tronto, professor of political science and women's studies at CUNY, discusses the philosophical underpinnings of this quandary in her work, an analysis of the morals and politics of caregiving. She writes:

> When we care, we do not think of society, we think of our intimates and their concrete and particular needs. In a competitive society, what it means to care well for one's own children is to make sure they have a competi-

tive edge against other children. On the most concrete level, while parents may endorse a principle of equality of opportunity in the abstract, their daily activities are most visibly "caring" when they gain special privileges and advantages for their children. Arguments about the value of universal public education and so forth, lose their force when they affect the possibility of *our* children's future.

Seen in this light, parental worrying is much more of a problem for society than it will ever be for individual children. In a society that is already competitive, the perception of more competition, or the magnification of competition through the lens of parental worrying, can only make things worse when worried parents are acting not as parents but as citizens.

Let's take the example of SUVs. America is once again involved in a debate about energy independence. This debate is not new, of course; in the 1970s we had to work toward energy independence to free ourselves from the machinations of OPEC. In the 2000s we have to work toward energy independence so that we can set limits with some of our less trustworthy allies in the war against terrorism—which is hard to do if we need their oil. Whether we achieve this goal through exploitation of domestic reserves or through conservation and innovation, everyone pretty much agrees that we need to be less dependent on foreign oil.

So, we need to drive more fuel-efficient cars. This is where parental worrying comes in. Articles in the public press inveigh against Americans' bizarre love affair with SUVs, sometimes derided as "urban assault vehicles," which are notoriously inefficient in terms of gas mileage. There is precious little analysis, in the public discussion of these issues, regarding exactly *why*, when we are supposed to be working on energy independence, everybody clings to their SUV. But there is often an absence of analysis in a situation where the truth is well known to everyone. The truth is, at least in my corner of the world, that *every-one with children drives the biggest car the family can possibly afford*. I do not know one family that happily drives children around in a plain old sedan or, God forbid, a compact car. The only people who do this are people who can't afford to drive a bigger car.

And everyone knows the reason for this. The reason is safety. The reasoning goes, I don't want my children to be mashed in an accident with another (huge, heavy) automobile. If there is an accident, I want my child or children to be safe. And the only way to be safe, in a world where everybody *else* has a big heavy car, is to have a big heavy car. Whether this is true is not the point (and there are some who suggest that it is not true that lighter cars are less safe); what matters is that every parent believes it to be true.

It might be that these are just the people I know. But let's listen to the experts. Marketing research performed by the now illustrious Dr. Clotilde Rapaille, a French medical anthropologist who has consulted to both DaimlerChrysler and Ford, suggests that SUVs are associated with the military, and with strength and power, and thus their appeal is primarily to people who are concerned with power: men who want to demonstrate their power and women who want to ward off criminals. Advertisements for SUVs (as opposed to the minivan, the ultimate carpooling vehicle) therefore appeal to these features of the SUV buyer: aggression, competitiveness, triumph over physical obstacles (the ad where the guy has to drive his Jeep Grand Cherokee Limited over a huge pile of rocks to get to his palatial home), and triumph over other people (the ad for the Lincoln Navigator featuring the motto "Ditch the Joneses"). These ads are not targeted just at parents, of course, but there is certainly an appeal to worried parents in the more general appeal to worried Americans who feel that they need to drive tanks to keep their families safe. In the debates about fuel efficiency standards in the U.S. Congress in March of 2002, Senator Christopher Bond (R-Missouri) stated on the floor of the Senate: "I don't want to tell a mom in my state that she should not get an SUV because Congress decided that would be a bad choice." In the same debate, Senator Trent Lott (R-Mississippi) held up a picture of a tiny purple car and derided this vehicle as the "car of the future" if the bill passed, while one of the bill's sponsors complained that fuel efficiency could be obtained without forcing Americans to drive smaller vehicles. In other words, *nobody,* including this bill's sponsors, would dream of committing the politically suicidal act of suggesting that Americans, especially moms, drive smaller cars: the only contest is between big cars that guzzle a lot of gas and big cars that guzzle less gas.

In such a world, energy efficiency does not stand a chance. It might be nice, it might be a societal good, to work toward energy independence and to stop global warming at the same time. But most parents simply will not participate in something they believe endangers their children. As long as everybody else is driving an SUV, parents will want a big heavy car, and if the war on terrorism and the global climate goes down the tubes, well, that's a darn shame. Until car designers can come up with cars that are fuel-efficient and are perceived to be safe for children,* the chunk of the population who are parents are not going to be converted to the cause of fuel efficiency.

Parental worrying is a powerful force that can drastically affect the actions of governments. When worrying is out of hand, governments are in danger of acting like anyone else who is really, really worried: in a wave of urgency, they are likely to take steps that will put an end to the worrying once and for all, or at least until the next wave of worry overtakes everyone. And parental worrying can serve up a trump card for politicians because if a particular policy is for children, it's pretty hard to oppose.

---

* It turns out that SUVs are not even all that safe, because of the threat of rollovers because of their height. But they look mighty safe, because they look like military vehicles.

And speaking of drastic action, let's take a moment to consider the effect of ongoing or prolonged worrying on individual parents. It is not fun; it produces, so to speak, wear and tear. When parents are in the throes of an important decision about their children's lives (like whether to go back to work) or in the throes of what may be a crisis in their children's lives (as when the children are apparently throwing off each and every yoke), they often feel stressed out, tired, and terrible about their own lives. They feel like failures. They feel like losers. They feel like people who should never have had children at all.

The thing about this condition is that people sometimes want to end it at all costs. It is a paradoxical, but true, fact about worried people that they often fret and obsess for weeks or months on end about a decision that they need to make, and then they make it impulsively. It does not seem that the decision could possibly be impulsive after all this consideration. But many people in this condition act in haste, not after reaching a satisfying decision to end all the obsessing but because they can't take it anymore. This way of ending worrying, while completely understandable, is not a good way to serve the interests of a family. And children are often confused by it; they don't see the worrying anyway, so it just looks as if they are being jerked around for no apparent reason.

A brief example: a parent who is worried about whether or not his child is taking drugs will frequently blame his child's companions. This is also understandable, because sometimes kids who are ready to experiment with drugs will hang around with other kids who are in the same state of mind. But as I noted in Chapter 6, companions are not usually the biggest problem. If a kid wants to get drugs, he will probably get drugs, and if he doesn't get them from his companions, he will get them from his own household in the form of alcohol, or prescription medications, or worse. But sometimes the worried parent feels that "something must be done," or "I can't just sit by and watch this happen." So the parent makes the decision to change schools for the child, or impulsively forbids the child to see friend X or Y or Z. This does nothing except make the parent feel that something has been done, and it sometimes works to alleviate worrying temporarily. But if the problem is that the child in question is straying into an adult-free zone too quickly because of some problems with feeling that authority is helpful, such action usually backfires. It simply demonstrates to the child in question that authorities are, not to put too fine a point on it, nuts. The parents demonstrate that they are arbitrary, hateful, clueless people who don't understand anything at all, including (from the child's point of view) that "I can get drugs anywhere at any time, so stopping me from seeing my friends is not going to make any difference."

Impulsive action can happen in the context of the family or in the context of school, with equally deleterious effects. Certainly in cases of scapegoating as a way of managing worrying, impulsive action can feel like the right thing to do at the time, but can ultimately backfire. If a child seems creepy, and there is a general feeling that "something must be done" to make the school community feel safer, the kid can be thrown overboard. But like the sacrifices made in the Salem witch trials, the community often comes to regret having made the impulsive decision to sacrifice one of its own. Parents and children who are involved in such a sacrifice are often left feeling temporarily assuaged, but ultimately guilty and still unsafe, because it is never clear who might be next.

In reality (if there is such a thing), parents often have much more time than they think to make a decision. In real emergencies, time is of the essence, but I hope that the foregoing chapters have shown that many of the things that feel like real emergencies where our children are concerned are not emergencies at all. Very frequently, my role as a child therapist and consultant to parents consists of simply giving parents permission to consider their options in a worry-free zone; and if that can be established, they often come to a decision that is truly satisfying, not because it temporarily ends the wear and tear of worrying, but because it is a decision that accords with the parents' own values. It becomes a right decision when it feels right, and it feels right when people take the time to examine who they are and who their children are, and to find a decision that meets the needs of both.

WORRIED PARENTS, IRONIC CHILDREN

But what about them? Surely there must be *some* effect on our children, who are the object of all this worrying. If it is true that today's parents are more cautious, or unsure, or neurotic, or equivocal, than ever before, this must be passed along somehow. I believe that there are some effects to look for, and while they are small, they are really there. We do know that a generalization about our children will not apply to all of them. A group of people in a generation or demographic group are individuals, and their individual differences are at least as important as any measurable characteristic spread out over a large population. But there might be some variables or traits that, if measured, might show that our children have higher scores on trait X or trait Y than we do, and these group differences may, at least in theory, be attributable to the effects of being raised by worried parents.

It needs to be said again here that, to my knowledge, this research has not been done in a systematic way. What we learned about children in small families is that the parents in such families are more worried than other parents, because they are by definition first-time parents for a greater period of time. The kids seem to turn out all right on measures of adjustment: school performance, citizenship, and motivation. But these studies have not measured every trait there is to measure, and we can speculate about the other traits that might be elevated in our children, who are being raised by people who believe that parenting now is harder than it has ever been.

Imagine, if you will, the effect of being looked at all the

time. Imagine that you are a first child whose worried parent is constantly checking on you to make sure you are still breathing. What would that be like? If the checking continued, and the worried first-time parent was pretty much always checking on you, peering at you, and looking at you for signs of illness, problem, or trauma, you might get used to being looked at, but you might adapt in some way to the experience of scrutiny. You might get used to attention to the surface, so to speak, or attention to your own outward presentation, and you might become very aware of yourself, and how you come across. You might become, in a word, self-conscious.

Now imagine that you are a grown-up at a party, and the party has had an awkward start. People have been milling around, not knowing what to say, introducing themselves but feeling uncomfortable because there have been a few too many silences in which nobody knows what is going to come next. Then, for some reason—maybe the food or the wine or the music—things loosen up, and everybody starts having a better time. People relax and start feeling less guarded about their presentation. And then, the host or hostess ruins it all by saying, "Oh, I'm so glad we're really having fun," or, "Isn't it nice that we can all be friends?" or some other awkward comment that once again calls attention to the fact that someone is evaluating the process—and everyone once again starts to feel terribly self-conscious.

Self-consciousness, the sense of watching and being watched, can spoil a party for grown-ups, and I believe that it can spoil a childhood for children as well. If you know, deep down, and with every neuron in your brain, that not just some but *every* picture you draw will end up plastered on the family's refrigerator, you might end up drawing differently. If *every* move you make is videotaped by Mom or Dad, every silly little song or dance routine, every event, no matter how small, every everything, you might develop a sense of being onstage a lot of the time. You might become more self-conscious than other people, or certainly more self-conscious than people who have been, at least some of the time, ignored. You become aware that everything you do, no matter how small, has enormous significance for the adults around you.

Being raised by worried parents gives children a sense of real power over adults. After the age when they have become aware of such things, children can start to feel like they can make or break a parent's day, week, or year. If a little expressed sadness or anger or failure on the part of the child can send Mom or Dad into a tizzy, sooner or later that child ends up knowing this, and censoring himself. If he then wants to send Mom or Dad into a tizzy, he can do so by reporting that things aren't going well. If, on the other hand, he is worried about Mom and Dad's obvious vulnerability, he can choose not to tell them what's really going on, because he can't trust them not to go into yet another tizzy.

Many parents express their own side of this transaction by worrying terribly about the after-school conversation; when asked, "How was school?" many kids will say, "Fine," or, "Okay," or nothing, and parents feel terribly worried because they have no data about their child's day. There are books on the subject that will give detailed instructions about how to create a climate in which children will really open up, and many parents who have consulted with me have read these books from cover to cover. *They want to know more.* Being involved parents, they want to know things in detail. They hunger for the quotidian data about their child's day in fourth grade.

I sometimes make parents angry by suggesting that they might, in fact, cultivate an attitude of wishing to know less. I don't mean by this that parents will really want to know less but rather that the worried inquiry itself, the expression of concern about "How was your day?" is sometimes so urgent and overwhelming that kids don't want to get into it. They just don't want to have every piece of data, everything they say, put through the worry mill, where it is evaluated as evidence for or against the child's well-being. It is just too much. It is too much power to have. It is too much to be able to ruin someone's day every day after school, to feel like Caesar, who with the power of a thumb going up or down can deprive people of (emotional) life.

I believe that children and adolescents are more ironic today than children used to be, and that includes current parents when they were children. The age of irony is now supposed to be past, now that the events of September 11 have infused our nation with a sense of larger purpose other than making money, and I, for one, hope fervently that this is so. But so far, no one has told our children and teenagers, who continue to live in an atmosphere of apparent mockery and insincerity in which demonstrating a real belief in something, or looking up to something or admiring something, is way deep down below the surface—and what's on the surface is an air of ironic detachment.

Adolescents have been allergic to phonies for at least several decades, but what sometimes feels different about today's adolescents is that they also include themselves on the phony list. Certainly for some of the decades of the last century, adolescent music and popular culture celebrated the idea of Diogenes: every teenager was a pure soul looking for truth in a world of hypocrites. Just take the evidence of popular song; imagine a world in which a song like Gene Pitney's 1961 hit "Town Without Pity" could be sung by a teenager with a straight face. It is unimaginable, at least to me, that such an earnest, self-pitying song could be done today. The contemporary style is to assert that the corruption of the young by adults is not a feared possibility, but an accomplished fact. Sometimes this fact is embraced with cheer, as it was by Madonna in "Material Girl" in 1984, and sometimes with rage, as in Limp Bizkit's 1999 hit "Break Stuff." But adolescents' claims to be idealistic victims of adults are long gone.

In therapy hours with child patients, I often hear issues of children's unnerving power stated with refreshing simplicity. "Why can't they leave me alone?" is a common refrain that might be heard in any era, but "I wish they had some other hobby besides me" strikes me as relatively new. If every act on the part of a child is greeted as if it were terribly momentous, the child has trouble making sense of what is trivial; is there anything that is trivial? A child needs freedom to create himself by trying out solutions, whether solutions to problems in drawing or solutions to problems in self-identification, and then rejecting the solutions that don't seem to work or make sense. But if every solution to every problem is kept, filed, analyzed, and thought about by a worried parent, the process is interfered with, in some subtle but important ways. And the result may be a defensive layering in which what is really important is kept hidden, so that it can develop without intrusion. The British child analyst D. W. Winnicott wrote beautifully of the necessity for a child to be quietly alone in the presence of the mother, as a condition of vital self-creation. What I often see in my clinical work is children who have never had this experience because a worried parent never leaves them alone. The surface becomes false, ironic, and self-mocking, while the real stuff—the stuff the child really cares about—continues on, but only deep underground.

In such a world, I sometimes try to recommend to parents something like benign neglect. Benign neglect is a concept that has a bad reputation, thanks to Richard Nixon, but it is a concept worth resurrecting in the field of parenting. If you are *quietly* available as a parent, the child can come to you to tell you what is important, and by implication, what is not. But if everything is too important, it is impossible to know what is really important, because there is no scale of value. In such cases, I have sometimes suggested to a parent that they get a dog—not for the child but for the parent. And sometimes it works—but sometimes the parent can ruin it by spending too much time taking pictures every time the child plays with the dog.

In the end, I do believe that most of our children will turn out just fine. This is something that I try to convey to people every day, with more or less success depending on the circumstances. The facts in this book, the data about the probability of disastrous outcomes, support this view: there are always dramatic instances to the contrary, but the facts suggest pretty strongly to me that many of our worries about our children now are greatly overblown.

But as I hope I have shown, this task is ultimately not about facts. This is about the weight one gives to the facts, the old feelings that attach themselves to the facts and amplify or distort them according to our own internal pressures. And when we spend all that time thinking about what we are doing or not doing to raise our children, we tend to forget that they are also involved in raising themselves.

Anyone who works with children knows about the extraordinary resources they bring to their own development—they need help, of course, but they also make themselves to an extraordinary degree. The view of parenting expressed in this book is, I hope, a simple one: kids need parents to love them and protect them and set limits with them, and they also need parents to get out of the way so that they can bring themselves up. This is hard to do in a world that seems dangerous and competitive and way too complicated, but it is still true. For families who do have choices, sometimes the array of choices may seem overwhelming, but eventually we need to give the choices to them to make. Trusting that they will make the right choices, or, if they make the wrong choices, that they will not be disastrous, is what we all have to do as parents. If these recommendations seem paradoxical, so be it. The best way to help them, I believe, is for us to know ourselves better. When we know ourselves better—our own values, our own sorrows, our own wishes for ourselves—we can look at them and know who they are and what they need, or don't need, from us.

They are paradoxical also because parenting is one of those things that really works when you stop trying so hard; most often, you can really be a good parent when you let go of the effort and stop worrying about the outcome. One last metaphor: parenting is like skating. Thinking about it is the first step, but it only takes you so far; then it's time to let go, to stop thinking about where each foot should go and what each muscle should do. And when you really let go, you can really enjoy it, because you can fly across the ice and experience freedom in a way that thinking about skating can never accomplish. When you have done all the thinking you need to do about your children, it's time to let go, trust yourself, and fly—and let your children fly along behind—and trust that whatever direction they go in, they'll have the ability to fly back.

NOTES

Introduction. Whose Zeitgeist Is It, Anyway?

5 *article with the lurid title:* Lucinda Franks, "The Sex Lives of Your Children," *Talk,* February 2000.

5 *story of two teenaged murderers:* Ron Powers, "The Apocalypse of Adolescence," *Atlantic Monthly,* March 2002.

5 *predicting the likelihood of violence:* T. Chiricos, S. Eschholz, and M. Gertz, "Crime, News and Fear of Crime: Toward an Identification of Audience Effects," *Social Problems* 44 (3): 342–57 (1997).

6 *annual incomes below the poverty line:* U.S. government poverty statistics obtained from the U.S. Census Bureau at www.census.gov.

6 People *magazine trumpeted:* "Bullies: The Disturbing Epidemic Behind School Violence," *People,* June 4, 2001.

7 *Public Agenda conducted a national telephone poll:* Steve Farkas and Jean Johnson, with Ann Duffett and Ali Bers, *Kids These Days: What Americans Really Think About the Next Generation* (Public Agenda, 1999).

9 *"Around me, the questions swirled":* Jon Katz, *Death by Station Wagon* (New York: Bantam Books, 1994), 112.

10 *"This 'Oh, my God, we're parents!' "*: David Kamp, "Oh, My God, We're Parents!" *GQ*, June 2000, 111–14.

One. Nervous Wrecks

21 *research published by pediatricians:* M. Klaus and J. Kennell, *Maternal-Infant Bonding: The Impact of Early Separation or Loss on Family Development* (St. Louis: Mosby, 1976).

22 *obsession with mother-infant bonding:* Diane Eyer, *Mother-Infant Bonding: A Scientific Myth* (New Haven: Yale University Press, 1992).

22 *"what every Dad needs to know":* William Sears, M.D., "Daddy Love," *Parenting,* June/July 2001, 78–83.

23 *academicians from the University of California:* Andrew Mecca, Neil Smelser, and John Vasconcellos, eds., *The Social Importance of Self-Esteem* (Berkeley: University of California Press, 1989).

24 *self-esteem movement was demolished:* William Damon, *Greater Expectations: Overcoming the Culture of Indulgence in Our Homes and Schools* (New York: Free Press, 1995); John P. Hewitt, *The Myth of Self-Esteem: Finding Happiness and Solving Problems in America* (New York: St. Martin's Press, 1998).

26 *overall trends are unmistakable:* Jason Fields and Lynne Casper, "America's Families and Living Arrangements: Population Characteristics," *Current Population Reports,* P20-537 (Washington: U.S. Census Bureau, 2001).

27 *what is now called evolutionary psychology:* Robert Trivers, "Parental Investment and Sexual Selection," in Lynne Houck and Lee C. Drickamer, eds., *Foundations of Animal Behavior: Classic Papers with Commentaries* (Chicago: University of Chicago Press, 1998).

28 *neglected, or even abused:* Jay Belsky, "Etiology of Child Maltreatment: A Developmental-Ecological Analysis," *Psychological Bulletin* 114 (3): 413–34 (1993). See also Robert Burgess and Alicia Drais, "Beyond the 'Cinderella Effect': Life History Theory and Child Maltreatment," *Human Nature* 10 (4): 373–98 (1999).

30 *House Majority Whip Tom DeLay:* DeLay's words, uttered on the floor of the U.S. House of Representatives, were widely reported. See Bob Herbert, "The True Believer," *New York Times,* Nov. 30, 2000.

31 *review of research on only children:* Toni Falbo and Denise Polit, "Quantitative Review of the Only Child Literature: Research Evidence and Theory Development," *Psychological Bulletin* 100 (2): 176–89 (1986).

31 *sleep through the night:* This research, from a number of sources, is summarized in Falbo and Polit, ibid.

33 *fussy, willful, and uncooperative:* Qicheng Jung, Chuanwen Wan, and Ray Over, "Single-Child Family in China: Psychological Perspectives," *International Journal of Psychology* 22 (1987): 127–38.

34 *identical twins:* David T. Lykken et al., "Heritability of Interests: A Twin Study," *Journal of Applied Psychology* 78 (4): 649–61 (1993).

Two. Dr. Schreber and Mrs. Jellyby

40 *"If you're a new parent":* Barbara Kantrowitz, "21st Century Babies," *Newsweek,* Fall-Winter 2000 Special Edition, "Your Child: Birth to Three," 4.

41 *particular child care environments:* William T. Greenough, "Experiential Modification of the Developing Brain," *American Scientist* 63 (1): 37–46 (1974).

42 *developmental psychologist Andrew Meltzoff:* Sharon Begley, "Wired for Thought," *Newsweek,* Fall-Winter 2000 Special Edition, 25.

43 *"The Science of Early Childhood Development":* Quoted ibid., 26.

43 *"I Am Your Child":* The I Am Your Child campaign, a nonprofit organization founded by actor and director Rob Reiner, is described fully on the campaign's Web site, www.iamyourchild.org.

43 *"media accounts":* Ross Thompson and Charles Nelson, "Developmental Science and the Media: Early Brain Development," *American Psychologist* 56 (1): 5–15 (2001).

45 *"Inside the Teen Brain":* U.S. News & World Report, August 8, 1999.

45 *kids who get less sleep:* Amy R. Wolfson and Mary Carskadon, "Sleep Schedules and Daytime Functioning in Adolescents," *Child Development* 69 (4): 875–87 (1998).

45 *simplistic response to a complicated question:* Mary Carskadon, personal communication, Feb. 7, 2002.

50 *"tyranny of choice":* Tyranny of choice is an idea popularized by Swarthmore professor Barry Schwartz in several speeches and in an upcoming book, *The Tyranny of Choice: When More Is Less.*

50 *consumers were forced to choose:* Sheena Iyengar and Mark Lepper, "When Choice Is Demotivating: Can One Desire Too Much of a Good Thing?" *Journal of Personality and Social Psychology* 79 (6): 995–1006 (2000).

52 *instinct and civilization:* S. Freud, *Civilization and Its Discontents,* trans. James Strachey (1939; reprint, New York: Norton, 1989).

53 not enough or too much: E. Erikson, *Childhood and Society* (New York: Norton, 1950).

53 *moderation as an effective parenting strategy:* Diana Baumrind, "The Discipline Controversy Revisited," *Family Relations: Journal of Applied Family and Child Studies* 45 (4): 405–14 (1996).

53 *Baumrind's original research:* Diana Baumrind, "Child Care Practices Anteceding Three Patterns of Preschool Behavior," *Genetic Psychology Monographs* 75 (1): 43–88 (1967). The data about parenting styles and high school student performance is contained in S. M. Dornbusch et al., "The Relation of Parenting Style to Adolescent School Performance," *Child Development* 58 (1987): 1244–57.

54 *corporal punishment is not an absolute evil:* Diana Baumrind, R. E. Larzelere, and Philip Cowan, "Ordinary Physical Punishment: Is It Harmful? Comment on Gershoff (2002)," *Psychological Bulletin* 128 (4): 580–89 (2002).

55 *development of personality disorders:* A. Golomb et al., "Maternal Empathy, Family Chaos and the Etiology of Borderline Personality Disorder," *Journal of the American Psychoanalytic Association* 42 (2): 525–48 (1994). Also see Marsha Linehan, *Cognitive-Behavioral Therapy of Borderline Personality Disorder* (New York: Guilford, 1993).

55 *adolescents with conduct disorders:* One example of this body of research is Carolyn Webster-Stratton, "Marital Conflict Management Skills, Parenting Style, and Early-Onset Conduct Problems: Processes and Pathways," *Journal of Child Psychology and Psychiatry and Allied Disciplines* 40 (6): 917–27 (1999).

55 *embroiled in their own developmental needs:* Marybeth Young, "Parenting During Mid-Adolescence: A Review of Developmental Theories and Parenting Behaviors," *Maternal-Child Nursing Journal* 17 (1): 1–12 (1988).

57 *New York Longitudinal Study:* Stella Chess and Alexander Thomas, *Temperament: Theory and Practice,* Brunner-Mazel Basic Principles into Practice Series, vol. 12 (London: Brunner-Routledge, 1996). See also Stella Chess and Alexander Thomas, *Goodness of Fit: Clinical Applications from Infancy Through Adult Life* (London: Brunner-Routledge, 1999).

Three. The Management of Worrying

72 *"A patient reported":* Aaron Beck, *Depression: Clinical, Experimental and Theoretical Aspects* (New York: Harper and Row, 1967), 235.

74 *skills of probability estimation:* Timothy Brown, Tracy O'Leary, and David Barlow, "Generalized Anxiety Disorder," in David H. Barlow, ed., *Clinical Handbook of Psychological Disorders* (New York: Guilford, 1993), 137–88.

75 *"This is the worst-case scenario":* Mark Jurkowitz, "Rink-Rage Trial Signals Return of Water-Cooler News," *Boston Globe,* Jan. 15, 2002.

76 *every other modern "threat":* Barry Glassner, *The Culture of Fear* (New York: Basic Books, 1999).

77 *Center for Risk Analysis:* Kimberly M. Thompson, "Kids at Risk," *Risk in Perspective* 8, no. 4 (2000). This online journal, published by the Harvard Center for Risk Analysis, may be found at www.hcra.harvard.edu.

Four. Oh, Those Nasty Date Books

86 *Americans work longer hours:* Juliet Schor, *The Overworked American: The Unexpected Decline of Leisure* (New York: Basic Books, 1991).

87 *" 'My son was 3 when I was told' ":* Ann Brochin, "Making the Grade: One Family's Adventure in Admissions," *Boston,* Oct. 2000, 78.

90 *"their children's 'anti-drugs' ":* "Kids Identify Family and Sports As Important Factors That Keep Them Away from Drugs" (Office of National Drug Control Policy Media Campaign, December 6, 2000).

90 The Hurried Child: David Elkind, *The Hurried Child: Growing Up Too Fast Too Soon,* 3rd ed. (Cambridge: Perseus, 2001).

98 *lifetime income associated with attending selective colleges:* Caroline Hoxby, "The Return to Attending a More Selective College: 1960 to the Present" (1999), available at www.economics.harvard.edu/faculty/hoxby.

99 *FBI statistics:* James Alan Fox et al., "America's After-School Choice: The Prime Time for Juvenile Crime or Youth Enrichment and Achievement" (2000), research report of Fight Crime: Invest in Kids, available at www.fightcrime.org.

99 *inadequate supervision of children:* David P. Farrington and Rolf Loeber, "Epidemiology of Juvenile Violence," *Child and Adolescent Psychiatric Clinics of North America* 9 (4): 733–48 (2000).

Five. Trouble in Au-Pairadise

106 *cross-cultural review of child-rearing practices:* Philippe Ariès, *Centuries of Childhood: A Social History of Family Life,* trans. Robert Baldrick (New York: Vintage, 1962); William Kessen, "The American Child and Other Cultural Inventions," *American Psychologist* 34 (10): 815–20 (1979).

107 *"In eighteenth-century Europe":* Jerome Kagan, *Three Seductive Ideas* (Cambridge: Harvard University Press, 1998), 85.

111 *"day care makes children more aggressive":* Jennifer Foote Sweeney, "The Day-Care Scare, Again," *Salon.com,* Apr. 20, 2001. See also Caryl Rivers, "Day-Care Report Launches Misinformed Hysteria," *Women's eNews,* Apr. 21, 2001.

118 *accusations of bad faith:* Cathy Young, "The Mommy Wars," *Reason,* July 2000.

118 *Abecedarian Project:* C. T. Ramey et al., "Persistent Effects of Early Intervention on High-Risk Children and Their Mothers," *Applied Developmental Science* 4 (2000): 2–14. The Abecedarian Project is described fully at www.fpg.unc.edu.

118 *National Institute of Child Health and Development:* The NICHD Study of Early Child Care is described at www.nichd.nih.gov/publications/pubs/early_child_care.htm.

124 *children who are killed:* "Variations in Homicide Risk During Infancy: U.S. 1989–1998," Morbidity and Mortality Report (U.S. Centers for Disease Control), March 8, 2002.

Six. Do As I Say, Not As I Did

132 *"the accumulation of unembarrassed insolence":* Adam Gopnik, "Blame Canada," *New Yorker,* Mar. 4, 2002, 29.

139 *covert adolescent wishes of parents:* Melvin Singer, "Delinquency and Family Disciplinary Patterns: An Elaboration of the Superego Lacunae Concept," *Archives of General Psychiatry* 31 (6): 795–98 (1974).

143 *the problem of adult authority:* George W. S. Trow, *Within the Context of No Context* (Boston: Little, Brown, 1981).

146 *nationwide survey of drug use by high school students:* "2001 Monitoring the Future Survey Released," *HHS News* (U.S. Department of Health and Human Services), December 19, 2001.

147 *addiction estimates for a population of adolescents and young adults:* J. C. Anthony, L. A. Warner, and R. Kessler, "Comparative Epidemiol-

ogy of Dependence on Tobacco, Alcohol, Controlled Substances and Inhalants: Basic Findings from the National Comorbidity Study," *Experimental and Clinical Psychopharmacology* 2 (1994): 244–68.

147 *Children and adolescents in mental health treatment settings:* G. Aarons et al., "Prevalence of Adolescent Substance Use Disorders Across Five Sectors of Care," *Journal of the American Academy of Child and Adolescent Psychiatry* 40 (4): 419–26 (2001).

Seven. Who's Afraid of the Big Bad Culture?

152 *Parents all over the world:* Benjamin Barber, *Jihad vs. McWorld* (New York: Ballantine, 1996).

154 *imitation as a way of knowing:* Jean Piaget, *Play, Dreams, and Imitation,* trans. C. Gattegno and F. M. Hodgson (New York: Norton, 1951).

159 *pioneers in television research:* Roni Tower et al., "Differential Effects of Television Programming on Preschoolers' Cognition, Imagination, and Social Play," *American Journal of Orthopsychiatry* 49 (2): 265–81 (1979).

159 *the orienting response:* Byron Reeves and Esther Thorson, "Watching Television: Experiments on the Viewing Process," *Communication Research* 13 (3): 343–61 (1986).

160 *metaphor of television as drug:* Marie Winn, *The Plug-in Drug* (New York: Penguin, 1985).

160 *how television works as an addictive activity:* R. Kubey and M. Csikszentmihalyi, "Television Addiction Is No Mere Metaphor," *Scientific American,* Feb. 2002, 74–80.

161 *After the introduction of television:* L. F. Harrison and T. M. Williams, "Television and Cognitive Development," in T. M. Williams, ed., *The Impact of Television: A Natural Experiment in Three Communities* (New York: Academic Press, 1986), 87–142.

165 *they're safer inside watching TV:* T. Chiricos, S. Eschholz, and M. Gertz, "Crime, News and Fear of Crime: Toward an Identification of Audience Effects," *Social Problems* 44 (3): 342–57 (1997).

167 *when they have their own televisions:* Most of the research about the deleterious effects of sheer quantities of television viewing (independent of content) has come from the pediatric community. This research was summarized in the position paper "Children, adolescents, and television," published by the American Academy of Pediatrics Committee on Public Education in *Pediatrics* 107 (2): 423–26 (2001).

See also V. C. Strasburger, "Does Television Affect Learning and School Performance?" *Pediatrician* 13 (2–3): 141–47 (1986).

168 *heavy exposure to television:* Susan Villani, "Impact of Media on Children and Adolescents: A 10-Year Review of the Research," *Journal of the American Academy of Child and Adolescent Psychiatry* 40 (4): 392–401 (2001).

168 *exposure to violent content in popular culture:* B. Bushman and C. Anderson, "Media Violence and the American Public: Scientific Facts Versus Media Misinformation," *American Psychologist* 56 (6–7): 477–89 (2001).

168 *report of the surgeon general:* David Satcher, *Youth Violence: A Report of the Surgeon General* (2001).

169 *"Suppose violent media":* B. Bushman and C. Anderson, "Media Violence and the American Public," 482.

170 *three hours every day watching TV:* This estimate is taken from the Nielsen Media Research 1998 Report on Television (New York: Nielsen Media Research).

Eight. When Columbine Was Only a Flower

175 *"A few days after the Columbine tragedy":* Elliot Aronson, *Nobody Left to Hate: Teaching Compassion After Columbine* (New York: W. H. Freeman, 2000).

180 *Experts who study youth violence:* E. Mulvey and E. Cauffman, "The Inherent Limits of Predicting School Violence," *American Psychologist* 56 (10): 797–802 (2001).

186 *strengthening the school community:* K. Howard, J. Flora, and M. Griffin, "Violence-Prevention Programs in Schools: State of the Science and Implications for Future Research," *Applied and Preventive Psychology* 8 (1999): 197–215.

186 *one big high school:* Meg Greenfield, *Washington* (New York: Public Affairs, 2001).

188 *healthy, fit offspring:* David Buss, *The Evolution of Desire: Strategies of Human Mating* (New York: Basic Books, 1994).

191 *fifty school-related violent deaths:* Statistics about youth violence obtained from the National Youth Violence Prevention Resource Center, www.safeyouth.org.

191 *homicides of youth:* Center for the Study and Prevention of Youth Violence at Colorado State University, www.colorado.edu/cspv.

Nine. But What About Them?

197 Boston Globe: Kate Zernicke, "Testing the Limits: A Pioneering Law Feels the Strain of Wide Demands," *Boston Globe,* Mar. 30, 1997.

197 *"diagnosis-shopping":* Jane Gross, "Paying for a Disability Diagnosis to Gain Time for College Boards," *New York Times,* Sept. 26, 2002.

198 *New York City suburb of Scarsdale:* Jane Gross, "A Binge by Teenagers Leads a Village to Painful Self-Reflection," *New York Times,* Oct. 7, 2002.

199 *"When we care":* Joan Tronto, "The Value of Care," *Boston Review* 27 (1): 16 (2002).

201 *Dr. Clotilde Rapaille:* Jack Hitt, "The Hidden Life of SUVs," *MoJoWire Magazine* (*Mother Jones Magazine* online version), July/Aug. 1999, available at www.motherjones.com.

202 *forcing Americans to drive smaller vehicles:* Richard Simon and Ronald Brownstein, "Senate Kills Stiffer Fuel Efficiency Standards," *Los Angeles Times,* Mar. 14, 2002.

202 *threat of rollovers:* "Rollover—The Hidden History of the SUV," PBS *Frontline* series. Research on SUV rollovers is available on the *Frontline* Web site at www.pbs.org/wgbh/pages/frontline/shows/rollover.

207 *a climate in which children will really open up:* Adele Faber and Elaine Mazlish, *How to Talk So Kids Will Listen and Listen So Kids Will Talk,* 20th anniversary ed. (New York: Avon, 1999).

209 *a condition of vital self-creation:* D. W. Winnicott, *The Maturational Processes and the Facilitating Environment: Studies in the Theory of Emotional Development* (New York: International Universities Press, 1965).

INDEX

accomplishments, 97–101
  facts about, 97–100
  nostalgia and, 84, 101
  overscheduling and, 87–93, 97–99,
    101
adolescents, adolescence, 69, 89, 115,
  208
  drug use and, 127–30, 132–33,
    138–41, 145–48
  exercises on, 149–50
  and meaning of cool, 131–34
  media and, 155–56, 158, 161
  during or after 1960s, 136–38
  problems with authority in,
    128–29, 131–33, 136–42,
    148–49
  scientific parenting and, 45–49,
    55
  sleep-wake cycles in, 45–48
  see also school violence

alcohol, 23–24, 164–65, 198
  addiction to, 147, 164
  experimenting with, 127–30,
    139–40, 148, 203
Alcoholics Anonymous (AA), 63–64,
  129–30
Anderson, Craig, 169
anxiety, 8*n*, 19, 56, 73, 83, 88
  definitions of, 67–68
  information overload and, 49–51
  national ebb and flow of, 21–25
  psychoanalysis and, 67–71
Aronson, Elliot, 175, 186–88
attachment theory, 108–9
attention, 35, 96
  media and, 165, 171
  scientific parenting and, 37–38
au pairs, 110, 120–22
authoritarianism, authoritarian
  parenting, 53–55, 113, 136

authoritative parenting, 53–54,
     136
authority:
   continuity and, 139, 142
   exercises on, 149–50
   fantasies about, 143–45
   and meaning of cool, 131–33, 143
   during or after 1960s, 136–38
   pathological integrity and, 138–43
   problems with, 128–29, 131–45,
     148–49, 204
   school violence and, 174, 181–82,
     184
autism, 57–58
automobiles:
   and effects of parental worrying,
     200–202
   seat belts and, 8, 77

Baumrind, Diana, 53–56
Beck, Aaron, 72–73
benign neglect, 209
Birds, The, 158
Bleak House (Dickens), 37–38
bonding, 21–23
brain, brain research, 115
   school violence and, 179–80
   scientific parenting and, 39–44,
     48–49
Brochin, Ann, 87
Bushman, Brad, 169

Carrie (King), 178
Carskadon, Mary, 45–48
Cauffman, Elizabeth, 180, 190
Chess, Stella, 57–59
child abductions, 75–76
children, child care:
   brutal facts on, 123–24
   effects of parental worrying on,
     194–200, 202, 205–9
   firstborn, 30–31, 34
   history of, 106–9
   importance of mothers to, 123

inborn temperaments of, 33–34,
     56, 58–60, 112–13, 141
   as ironic, 208–9
   only, 32–34, 94
   raising themselves, 210
   see also substitute care
China, family size in, 33
clarity paradox, 60–61
cliques, 186–88, 192
cognitive-behavioral therapies, 66,
     71–78, 80
college, colleges, 97–102, 137
   acceptance to, 88, 95, 97–100, 196,
     198
   accomplishments for, 88, 97–100
   applying to, 3, 69–70, 198
   and effects of parental worrying,
     196, 198
   exercises on, 101–2
   facts about, 97–100
   overscheduling and, 88, 95,
     97–100
Columbine incident, 19, 25, 173–76
   aftermath of, 30, 173–75, 178, 181,
     189
   discussion of cliques in, 186–87
   media coverage of, 169, 184
   number of deaths in, 191
   shooters in, 175, 187
competitiveness, competition, 26,
     117, 193, 210
   and applying to college, 69–70
   and effects of parental worrying,
     195–201
   family size and, 30, 35
   overscheduling and, 86, 88, 90,
     95–96, 100
computer literacy, 134–35
continuity, authority and, 139, 142
cool, coolness, 131–34, 143, 149
crime, criminals, 23–24, 169, 180,
     189, 195
   school violence and, 174–75, 181
   supervision and, 89, 99–100

Crouching Tiger, Hidden Dragon,
155
Csikszentmihalyi, Mihaly, 160–61,
166
Culture of Fear, The (Glassner),
76–78
cursing, media and, 151, 156, 162

Damon, William, 24
Dann, Marlene, 75
depression, 42, 50, 83
Beck on, 72–73
television and, 160–61, 166
developmental milestones, 124–25
substitute care and, 104–5, 112,
125
discipline, 38–39, 52, 72, 92
divorce, 56–57, 77–78
drug, drugs, 136
addiction to, 129–30, 147–48,
163–65
comparisons between television
and, 160–68, 171–72
experimenting with, 20, 23–24, 90,
127–30, 132–33, 138–48, 203–4
overscheduling and, 89–90, 92
pathological integrity and, 138–42
and problems with authority,
128–29, 132–33, 138, 142–45,
148, 204

early-childhood environments, 41,
43–44
empathy, 51, 55–57, 176
substitute care and, 111–14, 124
Erikson, Erik, 52–53
evolutionary theory, 109, 187–88
family size and, 27–30, 65
vigilance and, 65–66, 79

Falbo, Toni, 31–32
family size, family sizes, 194, 205
evolutionary theory and, 27–30, 65
and goodness of fit, 60

lived experience on, 27, 30–35
missing developmental milestones
and, 104–5
overscheduling and, 93–94, 96
parental worrying and, 26–36,
56
in past, 85
statistics on, 26–27, 30–32
substitute care and, 115–16
fantasies, 71, 80, 83–88, 178,
193
about adult authority, 143–45
media and, 161
nostalgia and, 83–87, 92, 95–96,
100–101
overscheduling and, 88, 92,
94–96
scapegoating and, 182–86
substitute care and, 109, 117,
122–23
fatherlessness, 77–78
freedom, 83, 87–94
Freud, Sigmund, 20, 39, 52
psychoanalysis and, 67, 74

Glassner, Barry, 76–78
goodness of fit, 51, 57–60
and authority, 141
and substitute care, 112–14,
124
guilt, 68–69, 93, 122, 199
authority and, 138, 145
scapegoating and, 204
school violence and, 182

Hamlet (Shakespeare), 70–71
Hewitt, John P., 24
honesty, 140–41
Hoxby, Caroline, 98–99

imitation, 154–57, 162, 168
impulsive parents, 203–5
infection metaphor, 152–53
information overload, 49–51

integrity:
  and effects of parental worrying,
    195–99
  pathological, 138–43, 190
Internet, 152, 168–70, 172, 195
  information overload and, 49–51
  scientific parenting and, 37, 40, 43,
    50–51
Iyengar, Sheena, 50

Jackson, Shirley, 184, 191

Kagan, Jerome, 107–9
Kamp, David, 9–10
Kantrowitz, Barbara, 40
Katz, Jon, 9
Kennell, John, 21–22, 44
Klaus, Marshall, 21–22, 44
Kubey, Robert, 160–61, 166

learning disabilities, 197–98
Lepper, Mark, 50
loneliness:
  overscheduling and, 93–94
  school violence and, 173–75,
    177–78, 180–81

Matrix, The, 155–56
media, media culture, 9–11, 19, 43,
    193, 200
  censorship of, 157, 161–63, 170
  on child abductions, 75–76
  and ebb and flow of national
    anxieties, 23, 25
  effects of exposure to, 14, 151–72
  open secrets about, 163–67
  pacing in, 158–62, 165–66, 170
  passivity in, 157–61, 169–70
  on rink rage father case, 74–75
  risk distortion in, 74–76
  on substitute care, 110–12
  on terrorism, 11, 152
  theatricality of, 154–56
  and treatment of worrying, 9–10

violence and, 157–58, 162, 167–70,
    180, 184
  vividness of, 154–58, 162
  youth worship and, 134–35, 142
  and zeitgeist of worrying, 4–7
  see also television, televisions
Memories of My Nervous Illness
    (Schreber), 38–39
meta-analysis, 31–32, 168
moderation, 51–54, 60
  scientific parenting and, 53–54
  substitute care and, 112–14, 124
Monitoring the Future study, 146–47
Mulvey, Edward, 180, 190

National Academy of Sciences, 42–43
National Institute of Child Health
    and Development (NICHD),
    118–19
National Institute on Drug Abuse
    (NIDA), 146
neglect, 41–42
Nelson, Charles, 43–44
New York Longitudinal Study
    (NYLS), 57–58
Nobody Left to Hate (Aronson), 175,
    186–87

Office of National Drug Control
    Policy (ONDCP), 89–90
overparenting, 4
overscheduling, 81–102
  complaints about, 82–83
  exercises on, 101–2
  facts about, 96–100
  fantasies and, 88, 92, 94–96
  nostalgia and, 83–87, 90–96,
    100–101
  parental choice in, 91–93, 100

parental investment, 27–30, 32–34
parents, parenting:
  comparisons between skating and,
    211

parents, parenting (*cont.*)
  effect of ongoing or prolonged
    worrying on, 203–5
  of firstborn children, 30–31, 34
  first-time, 31, 33, 205–6
  physical care in, 51–52
  projection in, 56–57, 68, 86,
    193–94
passivity:
  in media culture, 157–61, 169–70
  wise, 64–66, 78
permissiveness, permissive parenting,
    53–54, 113
plagiarism scandals, 195–96
Polit, Denise, 31–32
poverty, 6, 42, 77–78, 191
probability overestimation, 73–76
psychoanalysis, 39, 66–71, 74, 80
Public Agenda, 7, 194
punishment, punishments:
  and effects of parental worrying,
    195–96, 198–99
  moderation and, 53–54
  school violence and, 177, 183
  scientific parenting and,
    60–61
  whistleblowing and, 189–90

reading, reading skills, 47
  exercises on, 171–72
  media and, 157, 160, 170–72
rink rage father case, 74–75
risk assessment, 73–78, 80, 96

safety, 8, 91–92, 193–94, 210
  and effects of parental worrying,
    194, 201–2, 204
  media and, 164–65, 172
  nostalgia and, 84–85
  school violence and, 26, 174–76,
    178, 181–84, 190
  substitute care and, 108–10,
    120–23, 125
  supervision and, 89, 91

SATs, SAT scores, 13, 95, 99
  untimed, 196–97
scapegoating, 182–86, 204
school, schooling, 28, 45–49, 57,
    82–85, 131–32, 193
  drug use and, 127–28, 132,
    146–47, 204
  and effects of parental worrying,
    195–96, 198, 204–5, 207–8
  media and, 151, 156, 162, 167
  moderation and, 53–54
  nostalgia and, 84–85
  overscheduling and, 82–83, 87–93,
    99–102
  problems with authority in,
    132
  relationship between sleep and,
    45–46, 48
  scientific parenting and, 41–42,
    45–46, 49
  self-esteem in, 18–20, 24
  substitute care and, 103–5, 112,
    118, 125
  worries about, 17–21
school violence, 25–26, 173–92
  cliques and, 186–88
  exercises and, 191–92
  facts on, 190–91
  hitting in, 17, 19, 176
  national obsession with, 23, 25
  predictive factors for, 179–80
  prevention of, 174–85, 188–89,
    191–92
  rareness of, 179, 190–91
  risk distortion and, 76–77
  scapegoating and, 182–86,
    204
  teasing in, 6, 174–75, 177–78, 181,
    187
  verbal threats in, 173–74, 181
  whistleblowing and, 189–90
  see also Columbine incident
Schreber, Daniel Gottlieb Moritz,
    38–39, 44

scientific parenting, 13, 37–61
  brain research and, 39–44,
    48–49
  clarity paradox and, 60–61
  empathy and, 55–57
  and goodness of fit, 57–60
  history of, 38–39, 44
  information overload and, 49–51
  moderation and, 53–54
  values and, 44, 46–49, 51
self-consciousness, 206–7
self-esteem, 90, 100
  national obsession with, 23–24
  in school, 18–20, 24
self-reflection, 70–71
self-sacrifice, 64–65
separation process, 148–49
Serenity Prayer, 63–65
Sesame Street, 159, 170
sex, sexuality, 65, 68, 140
  media and, 5, 167, 170
  during or after 1960s, 136–37
  in school, 18, 20–21
sexual abuse, 18, 20–21, 110
  national obsession with, 23–24
Singer, Jerome and Dorothy,
    159
sleep, 31, 78, 167
  scientific parenting and, 45–48,
    59–61
smoking, 129, 148, 168
  addiction to, 163–64
society, socialization, social policies,
    8, 74, 107, 176–77, 186–87,
    191, 208
  authority and, 133, 144, 148
  effects of parental worrying on, 14,
    194–96, 199–202
  family size and, 30, 32–33, 34
  media and, 154, 162–63, 169
  moderation and, 51–54
  overscheduling and, 86, 88–89
  pathological integrity and, 142
  risk distortion and, 76, 78

school violence and, 173–74, 177,
    180, 187
  substitute care and, 116–17
stimulation:
  media and, 158–60, 164, 166, 170
  scientific parenting and, 41–43
substitute care, 103–25
  and ability to wait, 115–18, 120–21
  au pairs and, 110, 120–22
  dangers and, 108–10, 120–23, 125
  exercises on, 124–25
  financial cost of, 120–23, 125
  in group settings, 110, 114–21, 125
  logic of, 112–17
  missing developmental milestones
    and, 104–5, 112, 125
  in past, 108–9
  provider-to-child ratios in, 116,
    118–20
  research on, 112, 118–20
  specialness in, 117, 120, 122,
    125
  vigilance and, 79–80
  worries associated with, 110–12,
    119–20, 122–23
supervision, 85–87, 132, 137
  facts about, 99–100
  nostalgia and, 85–86
  overscheduling and, 87, 89–94, 97,
    99–101
SUVs, 200–202
Swartz, Steven, 10

teasing, 6, 174–75, 177–78, 181, 187,
    192
technology, 35–36, 134–35
television, televisions:
  in children's rooms, 167–68
  comparisons between drugs and,
    160–68, 171–72
  effects of program content of,
    162–63, 167, 169–71
  for instant relief, 164–68
  safety and, 164–65

terrorism, 11–13, 144, 208
  media on, 11, 152
  war against, 200, 202
Thomas, Alexander, 57–59
Thompson, Ross, 43–44
Three Seductive Ideas (Kagan),
  107
toy guns, 3–4
Trivers, Robert, 27
Tronto, Joan, 199–200
Trow, George W. S., 143–45
truth torturing, 198–99
Type I errors, 177–79

values, 64, 66, 209–10
  and effects of parental worrying,
    205, 209
  media and, 152–53
  and problems with authority, 133
  scientific parenting and, 44, 46–49,
    51
  substitute care and, 114, 117,
    121
  whistleblowing and, 189–90

vigilance, 65–66, 78–80, 194
violence:
  media and, 157–58, 162, 167–70,
    180, 184
  toy guns and, 3–4
  see also crime, criminals; school
    violence

whistleblowing, 189–90
Within the Context of No Context
  (Trow), 143–45
Woodward, Louise, 110, 120–22
worries, worrying, worriers:
  characteristics of, 73
  as overblown, 210
  polls on, 7–8
  as secular form of praying, 79
  treatment of, 8–11, 13–14, 66–80,
    96, 106, 107*n*, 122
  true stories on, 17–21
  zeitgeist of, 2–8, 18–19, 25–26

youth sports, 74–75
youth worship, 134–35, 141–42

ABOUT THE AUTHOR

David Anderegg, Ph.D., is a professor of psychology at Bennington College and has been treating children and families in psychotherapy for more than twenty years. Since 1994 he has also been the mental health consultant to the Berkshire Country Day School. He received his Ph.D. from Clark University and trained as a therapist at the Child Psychiatry Unit at Beth Israel Hospital in Boston. Anderegg lives in West Stockbridge, Massachusetts, with his wife and two college-age children.